SPEAK AND WRITE IN BETTER ENGLISH

SPEAK AND WRITE
IN
BETTER ENGLISH

By
DR. SHAILENDRA GOSWAMI

ANMOL PUBLICATIONS PVT. LTD.
NEW DELHI - 110 002 (INDIA)

ANMOL PUBLICATIONS PVT. LTD.
4374/4B, Ansari Road, Daryaganj
New Delhi - 110 002
Ph.: 23261597, 23278000
Visit us at: www.anmolpublications.com

Speak and Write in Better English

First Edition, 2002

Reprint, 2004

PRINTED IN INDIA

Published by J.L. Kumar for Anmol Publications Pvt. Ltd., New Delhi - 110 002 and Printed at Mehra Offset Press, Delhi.

Contents

A MESSAGE TO THE STUDENTS....

Dear Students,

In today's competitive world, who is not aware of the powers and potentials of a person well equipped with a powerful vocabulary ?

A good vocabulary is the power that enables a man surmount all the obstacles in his path. It is the essence of achievements and recognition.

Impressive vocabulary makes one's personality powerful and it is an attractive and powerful personality that enables one to achieve the much coveted echelons of prestige and power.

A good vocabulary leads to success in interviews, better marks in examinations, respect, recognition, better job, better salary, better business dealings and lots more. Undoubtedly, vocabulary is the strongest foundation of an impressive personality. This is the reason why you should crave to possess this dynamic power.

It is not difficult to have a good vocabulary. It is rather easy. Just give 15-30 minutes daily to this book—that's all. If you do this, each day you will find yourself rising faster and faster towards perfection—and success will soon touch your feet.

Wishing you all the best

Yours

PRONUNCIATION KEY

SYMBOL Vowels	EXAMPLE
æ	hat[hæt]
ə	across [ə'kros]
e	get [get]
I	hit [hit]
^	fun [f^n]
ʊ	put [pʊt]
o	pot [pot]
	dot [dot]
a:	harm [h*a*:m]
i:	he [hi:]
u:	too [tu:]
ɔ:	law [lɔ:]
ɜ:	sir [sɜ: (r)]
eI	say [seI]
aI	sky [skaI]
Iə	fear [fIə(r)]
eə	fair [feə(r)]
ɔI	toy [tɔI]
əʊ	go [gəʊ]
aʊ	now [naʊ]
ʊə	poor [pʊə(r)]

CONSONANTS

b, d, f, h, k, l, m, n, p, r, s, t, v, w and z have their usual pronunciation.

g -- gift [gift]

η -- sing [sɪη]

ʃ -- show [ʃəʊ]

θ -- throw [θrəʊ]

3 -- precision [prɪsɪz (ə)n]

j -- yes [jes]

tʃ -- chop [tʃop]

d_z -- jug [d_z^g]

(r) -- fear [fiə(r)]

(the (r) should be pronounced only when the word that follows begins with a vowel, e.g.fear of ... etc.

(ə) mettle ['met(ə)I]
sudden ['s^d(ə)n]

[(ə) is an indeterminate ə like sound]

STRESS

The main syllable to be stressed is preceded by the symbol '. the secondary syllable to be stressed is preceded by the symbol,.

PART ONE

It pays to know more...

ASSIGNMENT ONE. . . NOUNS

Lesson One

[A] Speak aloud the following words five times each.

	Words	Pronunciations
1.	Collaboration	kəlæbə`reIʃ(ə)n
2.	Enthusiasm	In`θju:zi,æz(ə)m
3.	Esteem	I`sti:m
4.	trepidation	,trepi`deiʃ(ə)n
5.	Confrontation	,konʃrʌnteiʃ(ə)n
6.	Adversary	`ædvəsərI

[B] Meanings and usage

1. **Collaboration:** Collaboration means 'union of people or parties to do some work with mutual co-operation and understanding'.
   - **Sentence:** Business collaborations yield higher profits.
   - **Your sentence:** ....

     ....

2. **Enthusiasm** : It means 'great eagerness or interest'.

   Sentences:

   - Shakespeare's enthusiasm in plays made him world famous.
   - Bindu has an insatiable enthusiasm in reading ghost stories.

- **Your sentence:**..

....

3. **Esteem:** Esteem means 'great respect'.

- **Sentences:** Mother Teresa's high personal esteem engenders awe and respect.

[engenders : gives birth to ...]

Every politician wants to achieve the highest position of esteem and power.

- **Your sentence:**..

....

4. **Trepidation:** Trepidation is a feeling of great fear or alarm that makes one tremble.

- **Sentence:** With trepidation Julie entered the thick forest in the dark night.
- **Your sentence:**..

....

5. **Confrontation:** Confrontation means 'a face-to-face' or 'front-to-front' meeting.

- **Sentence:** I had a confrontation with my enemy last night.
- **Your sentence:**..

....

6. **Adversary:** Adversary is an opponent.

- **Sentence:** Never fear your adversary if you want to win a battle.
- **Your sentence:**..

....

[C] Match the words in 'column A' with their meanings in 'column B'.

	Column A		Column B
1.	Collaboration	(a)	great eagerness or interest.
2.	Enthusiasm	(b)	dealing with, or facing a condition or opponent 'front-to-front'.
3.	Esteem	(c)	great respect
4.	Trepidation	(d)	feeling of fear or alarm
5.	Confrontation	(e)	union of people or parties to do some work with mutual understanding and co-operation.
6.	Adversary	(f)	an opponent.

Answers : 1-e; 2-a; 3-c; 4-d; 5-b; 6-f;

Lesson Two

[A] Speak aloud the following words five times each.

	Words	Pronunciations
1.	Obstacle	\`obstək(ə)l
2.	Strife	straɪf
3.	Apprehension	,æprɪ\`henʃ(ə)n
4.	Convocation	,konvə'keɪʃ(ə)n
5.	Sanctity	\`sæŋktɪtɪ
6.	Avarice	\`ævərɪs
7.	Malpractice	mæl\`præktɪs

[B] Usage practice

1. OBSTACLE:

- **Meaning:** Hindrance ; difficulty.
- **Sentence:** Intelligently Jane cleared all the obstacles in her path.
- **Your sentence:** ....

....

2. STRIFE:

- **Meaning:** Struggle
- **Sentence:** A prime minister's life is full of strife.

- **Your sentence:** ....

  ....

3. APPREHENSION:

- **Meaning:** Uneasiness mixed with anxiety.
- **Sentence:** Huge debt and collapsing business filled him with apprehension.
- **Your sentence:** ....

  ....

4. CONVOCATION:

- **Meaning:** A large formal gathering of people.
- **Sentence:** I attended a convocation of doctors last month.
- **Your sentence:** ....

  ....

5. SANCTITY:

- **Meaning:** Sacredness.
- **Sentence:** Quacks are tarnishing the sanctity of medical profession.
- **Your sentence:** ....

  ....

[Tarnish : to stain, or lessen the brightness of something by staining it]

6. AVARICE:

- **Meaning:** greed for wealth or money.
- **Sentences:** • Avarice kills one's moral values.
- Avarice engenders corruption and crime.
- **Your sentence:** ....

  ....

7. **MALPRACTICE:**

- **Meaning:** An immoral, bad, and unethical practice.

[unethical means against the principles or morals of a profession]

- **Sentence:** Malpractice in medical profession is tarnishing it's reputation.
- **Your sentence:** ....

....

[C] Match the words in 'column A' with their meanings in 'column B'.

	Column A		*Column B*
1.	Obstacle	(a)	A large formal gathering
2.	Strife	(b)	hindrance
3.	Apprehension	(c)	sacredness
4.	Convocation	(d)	struggle
5.	Sanctity	(e)	greed
6.	Avarice	(f)	uneasiness mixed with anxiety
7.	Malpractice	(g)	immoral practice

Answers: 1-b; 2-d; 3-f; 4-a; 5-c; 6-e; 7-g;

[D] Write down the words you have learnt in this chapter in front of their meanings.

1. Hindrance :..
2. Struggle : ....
3. Uneasiness mixed with anxiety :....................................
4. A large formal gathering :..

5. Sacredness : ....

6. Immoral and unethical practice : ....

7. Greed for money or wealth : ....

Answers : 1-Obstacle ; 2-Strife ; 3-Apprehension; 4-Convocation; 5-Sanctity; 6-Malpractice; 7-Avarice

Lesson Three

[A] Speak aloud the following words five times each.

	Words	*Pronunciations*
1.	Debacle	deɪ`ba:k(ə) l
2.	Tenacity	tI`næsItI
3.	Controversy	`kontrə,v3:sI
4.	Crusade	kru:`seId
5.	Chaos	`keIos

[B] Usage practice

1. DEBACLE:

- **Meaning:** A complete failure
- **Sentence:** The inexperienced youth faced an embarrassing debacle in establishing a new factory.
- **Your Sentence:** ....

....

2. TENACITY:

- **Meaning:** not appropriate; persistence.
- **Sentence:** His tenacity in learning computers has made him the most respected computer engineer in this region.
- **Your Sentence:** ....

....

3. **CONTROVERSY:**

- **Meaning:** A prolonged dispute, or difference in opinion.
- **Sentence:** Whether the egg came first or the hen, is a matter of controversy.
- **Your Sentence:** ....

....

4. **CRUSADE:**

- **Meaning:** A fierce campaign or war.
- **Sentence:** A deadly crusade is going on between the two powerful countries.
- **Your Sentence:** ....

....

5. **CHAOS:**

- **Meaning:** Disorder and confusion.
- **Sentence:** The terrible bomb explosion resulted in an uncontrollable chaos.
- **Your Sentence:** ....

....

[C] Match the following:

Words	*Meanings*
1. Debacle	(a) prolonged dispute
2. Tenacity	(b) disorder and confusion
3. Controversy	(c) a complete failure
4. Crusade	(d) a fierce campaign
5. Chaos.	(e) persistence.

Answers : 1-c, 2-e; 3-a; 4-d; 5-b

[D] Can you recall the words you have learnt in this chapter ?

1. D__ __ __ C __ __ (a complete failure)
2. T __ __ __ C __ __ __ (persistence).
3. C__ __ T __ __ V __ __ __ __ (difference in opinion)
4. C__ __ O __ (disorder and confusion).
5. C__ __ S __ __ __ (A fierce campaign or war).

Answers : 1-debacle ; 2-tenacity ; 3-controversy; 4-chaos; 5-crusade

Lesson four

[A] Speak aloud the following words five times each.

	Words	*Pronunciations*
1.	Conflict	\`konflɪkt
2.	Aspect	\`æspekt
3.	Compromise	\`komprə,maɪz
4.	Scenario	sɪ′na:rɪəu
5.	Opportunity	,opə\`tju:nɪtɪ
6.	Bibliophile	\`bɪblɪəʊ,faɪl

[B] Usage practice

1. **CONFLICT:**
   - **Meaning:** a fight or dispute.
   - **Sentence:** "The increasing number of internal conflicts will ruin this company," said the manager.
   - **Your Sentence:** ....
     ....
2. **ASPECT:**
   - **Meaning:** A view of something from one angle or direction.
   - **Sentence:** "You see only the emotional aspect of love marriage, not the practical one", the old man shouted in anger.

- **Your Sentence:** ....

  ....

3. **COMPROMISE:**

- **Meaning:** Settlement or agreement reached by deductions or sacrifice from either side.
- **Sentence:** Compromises settle many disputes and solve many problems.
- **Your Sentence:** ....

  ....

4. **SCENARIO:**

- **Meaning:** Outline of a scene.
- **Sentence:** In the present day scenario, humanity can be seen suffering at every nook and corner.
- **Your Sentence:** ....

  ....

5. **OPPORTUNITY:**

- **Meaning:** a chance.
- **Sentence:** An intelligent man never misses a good opportunity.
- **Your Sentence:** ....

  ....

6. **BIBLIOPHILE:**

- **Meaning:** One who loves books.
- **Sentence:** Capricornians are said to be great bibliophiles.
- **Your Sentence:** ....

  ....

[C] Match the following

	Words		***Meanings***
1.	Conflict	(a)	a view from one angle.
2.	Aspect	(b)	outline of events or scene
3.	Compromise	(c)	a fight or dispute
4.	Scenario	(d)	a chance
5.	Opportunity	(e)	settlement reached by sacrifice
6.	Bibliophile	(f)	A lover of books.

Answers : 1-c; 2-a; 3-e; 4-b; 5-d; 6-f

Lesson Five

[A] Speak aloud the following words five times each

	Words	*Pronunciations*
1.	Agenda	ə`dzendə
2.	Slump	slʌmp
3.	Hegemony	hɪ`dzemənɪ
4.	Norm	nɔ:m
5.	Defiance	di`faɪəns
6.	Disdain	dɪs`deɪn

[B] Let us practice the usage of these words now

1. **AGENDA:**
   - **Meaning:** a series of works to be done.
   - **Sentence:** A well planned agenda helps a lot in completing one's works within specified time limits.
   - **Your Sentence:** ....

     ....

2. **SLUMP:**
   - **Meaning:** a sudden severe downfall (especially in price or value of something).
   - **Sentence:** Today India is desperately trying to come out of the economic slump.

- **Your Sentence:** ....

  ....

3. **HEGEMONY:**

- **Meaning:** Leadership or authority, especially of one state of a confederacy* over others.
- **Sentence:** Some states try to seek hegemony over others to get some advantages.
- **Your Sentence:** ....

  ....

4. **NORM:**

- **Meaning:** a standard or a pattern.
- **Sentence:** Norms specified by Government must be strictly followed.
- **Your Sentence:** ....

  ....

5. **DEFIANCE:**

- **Meaning:** Open, bold and stubborn disobedience.
- **Sentence:** The defiance of the student was strictly punished by the principal.
- **Your Sentence:** ....

  ....

6. **DISDAIN:**

- **Meaning:** A mixed feeling of superiority, pride and hatred for others.
- **Sentence:** Rahul treats his wife with disdain.
- **Your Sentence:** ....

  ....

[* Confederacy is a union of states joined or allied to each other by treaty etc.]

[C] Match the following:

	Words		*Meanings*
1.	Agenda	(a)	a sudden severe downfall
2.	Slump	(b)	a standard or a pattern.
3.	Hegemony	(c)	a series of things to be done.
4.	Norm	(d)	open and bold disobedience.
5.	Defiance	(e)	leadership, especially by one state of a confederacy over others.
6.	Disdain.	(f)	a feeling of superiority, pride, and dislike for others.

Answers : 1-c; 2-a; 3-e; 4-b; 5-d; 6-f;

[D] Can you spell correctly the words you have learnt in this chapter ? Write the words in the space provided below and check whether you have spelt them correctly or not.

1. A series of works to be done : A ....
2. A sudden severe downfall : S ....
3. Leadership by one state or a confederacy over others : H ....
4. A standard or a pattern : N ....
5. Open, bold and stubborn disobedience : D ....
6. A feeling of pride and superiority, with dislike for others. : D ....

Answers : 1-Agenda; 2-Slump; 3-Hegemony; 4-Norm; 5-Defiance; 6-Disdain.

Lesson Six

[A] Speak aloud the following words five times each

Words	*Pronunciations*
1. Envoy	\`envɔɪ
2. Endurance	ɪn\`djʊərəns
3. Perspective	pe\`spektɪv
4. Perseverance	,pɜ:sɪ\`vɪərəns
5. Proliferation	prəlɪfə'reɪʃ(ə)n
6. Assassin	ə\`sæsɪn

[B] Usage practice

1. ENVOY:
   - **Meaning:** a representative (for diplomatic dealings).
   - **Sentence:** The envoys from different countries met in the convocation to discuss the political matters.
   - **Your Sentence:** ....

     ....

2. ENDURANCE:
   - **Meaning:** Tolerance
   - **Sentence:** Indian women have remarkable endurance.
   - **Your Sentence:** ....

     ....

3. **PERSPECTIVE:**

- **Meaning:** A view regarding relative importance of things.
- **Sentence:** Only a person with a balanced perspective can run a big business successfully.
- **Your Sentence:** ....

....

4. **PERSEVERANCE:**

- **Meaning:** Continuous or sustained persistence.
- **Sentence:** Despite multiple failures, Bindu never got discouraged. Ultimately she succeeded in getting a job in the medical college. It is true, perseverance always pays.
- **Your Sentence:** ....

....

5. **PROLIFERATION:**

- **Meaning:** Rapid multiplication: rapid increase in number.
- **Sentence:** The proliferation of crime must be checked immediately.
- **Your Sentence:** ....

....

6. **ASSASSIN:**

- **Meaning:** A murderer (especially of an important person).
- **Sentence:** The assassins, who murdered our prime minister, have been punished by law, said the reporter.
- **Your Sentence:** ....

....

(C) Match the following

	Words		*Meanings*
1.	Envoy	(a)	A view regarding relative importance of things.
2.	Endurance	(b)	Ability to tolerate
3.	Perspective	(c)	A representative.
4.	Perseverance	(d)	Rapid multiplication or increase in number
5.	Proliferation	(e)	A murderer especially of an important person.
6.	Assassin	(f)	Sustained, continuous persistence.

Answers: 1–c; 2–b; 3–a; 4–f; 5–d; 6–e.

(D) Can you recall the words you have learnt in this chapter? Let us see...

1. E ....
2. E ....
3. P ....
4. P ....
5. P ....
6. A ....

Lesson Seven

TEST YOUR PROGRESS

Students, first revise exercise 'B' of all the chapters in this assignment before taking this test. It will hardly take half an hour, and would help you score very high in this test.

[A] Match the following

Words		*Meanings*
1. Collaboration	(a)	great respect
2. Esteem	(b)	hindrance
3. Trepidation	(c)	to stain, or lessen the brightness of (by staining).
4. Obstacle	(d)	a feeling of fear or alarm.
5. Strife	(e)	a large formal gathering.
6. Convocation	(f)	persistence
7. Sanctity	(g)	a union of people or parties to do a work with mutual co-operation and understanding.
8. Tarnish	(h)	sacredness
9. Tenacity	(i)	struggle
10. Crusade	(j)	a long and fierce war (to protect a noble cause)

[B] Select the most appropriate word from the following to fill the blanks.

1 Enthusiasm 2. Confrontation 3. Debacle 4. Chaos 5. Scenario 6. Opportunity 7. Slump 8. Defiance 9. Endurance 10. Proliferation.

1. The .... of crime is a matter of great concern for the Government. [Hint: rapid multiplication]
2. In today's .... everyone is running after money. [Hint: an outline of a scene]
3. It was a very good ....! [Hint: chance]
4. The inexperienced youth had to face an embarrassing .... [Hint: complete failure]
5. I hate .... with my enemies. [Hint: meeting front-to-front].
6. The bomb explosion created a .... in the market place. [Hint: disorder and confusion].
7. He joined the new job with amazing .... [Hint: great interest or eagerness].
8. Indians are famous for their .... [Hint: tolerance].
9. The economic .... has weakened the country. [Hint: a sudden, severe downfall in value].
10. The child's .... was severely punished by the teacher. [Hint: open, bold and stubborn disobedience].

Answers:

[A] 1-g; 2-a; 3-d; 4-b; 5-i; 6-e; 7-h; 8-c; 9-f; 10-j.

[B] 1-proliferation; 2-scenario; 3-opportunity; 4-debacle; 5-confrontation; 6-chaos; 7-enthusiasm; 8-endurance; 9-slump; 10-defiance.

Calculate Your Marks

Give yourself one mark (+1) for each correct answer, and add them up to get your score.

Let us grade your performance now.

Marks obtained	**Remarks**
16-20	Excellent!
14-15	Very good
11-13	Good
8-10	Fair
6-7	Average
below 6	Poor.

Write the remark you got in this test in BOLD CAPITAL LETTERS with RED SKETCH PEN in the circle provided below.

This is the remark our student got in this test which indicates how he/she is progressing through this course.

Words shape your personality...

ASSIGNMENT TWO. . . VERBS

Lesson One

[A] Speak aloud the following words five times each

	Words	***Pronunciations***
1.	Rejuvinate	rɪ'dzu:vɪ,neɪt
2.	Epitomise	ɪ'pɪtə, maɪz
3.	Evoke	ɪ'vəʊk
4.	Deplete	dɪ'pli:t
5.	Ensue	ɪn'sju:

[B] Usage practice

1 REJUVINATE:

- **Meaning:** To make youthful again.
- **Sentence:** The success was enough to rejuvinate his strength after the great exhaustion.
- **Your Sentence:** ....

....

2. EPITOMISE:

- **Meaning:** This word is derived from 'epitome' [pronounce it as i`pitəmi:] which means 'a typical example of something'. So the word 'epitomise 'means' 'to exemplify.'
- **Sentence:** The Oxford University epitomises perfection in education.

- **Your Sentence:** ....

   ....

3. **EVOKE:**
   - **Meaning:** To bring forth (a response, etc.)
   - **Sentence:** It is difficult to evoke a positive response from stubborn children.
   - **Your Sentence:** ....

     ....

4. **DEPLETE:**
   - **Meaning:** To empty; exhaust.
   - **Sentence:** The days of continuous work have depleted my energy.
   - **Your Sentence:** ....

     ....

5. **ENSUE:**
   - **Meaning:** To follow [e.g. to follow as a result or sequelae of something].
   - **Sentence:** Many problems have ensued due to the carelessness of the authorities.
   - **Your Sentence:** ....

     ....

[C] Match the following

Words		*Meanings*
1. Rejuvinate	a.	to empty.
2. Epitomise	b.	to make youthful again.
3. Evoke	c.	to exemplify.
4. Deplete	d.	to follow.
5. Ensue	e.	to bring forth.

Answers: 1-b; 2-c; 3-e; 4-a; 5-d.

[D] Write the words you have learnt in this chapter in front of their meanings

1. To make youthful again : ....
2. To exemplify : ....
3. To bring forth : ....
4. To empty : ....
5. To follow : ....

Answers: 1-rejuvinate; 2-epitomise; 3-evoke; 4-deplete; 5-ensue.

Lesson Two

[A] Speak aloud the following words five times each

	Words	*Pronunciations*
1.	Demarche	dei'ma:ʃ
2.	Urge	3:dz
3.	Refrain	rɪ'freɪn
4.	Deteriorate	dɪ'tɪərɪə,reɪt.
5.	Integrate	'ɪntɪ,greɪt
6.	Abscond	əb'skond

[B] Let us practise the usage of these words now

1. DEMARCHE:

- **Meaning:** To take steps (especially political steps).
- **Sentence:** The Prime Minister démarched to secure his position in the country.
- **Your Sentence:** ....

  ....

2. URGE:

- **Meaning:** To ask earnestly.
- **Sentence:** I urged my boss to give me leave, but he refused.
- **Your Sentence:** ....

  ....

3. **REFRAIN:**
   - **Meaning:** To prevent someone from doing something.
   - **Sentence:** My father has refrained me from smoking cigarettes.
   - **Your Sentence:** ....

     ....
4. **DETERIORATE:**
   - **Meaning:** To make worse.
   - **Sentence:** Begging deteriorates one's position and reputation.
   - **Your Sentence:** ....

     ....
5. **INTEGRATE:**
   - **Meaning:** To add or combine.
   - **Sentence:** The scientists integrated all their resources to develop the new satellite.
   - **Your Sentence:** ....

     ....
6. **ABSCOND:**
   - **Meaning:** To run away secretly (especially to avoid punishment, duty, etc.).
   - **Sentence:** The criminal absconded soon after murdering the couple.
   - **Your Sentence:** ....

     ....

[C] Write the words you have learnt in this chapter in front of their meanings

1. To take steps (esp. political): ....

2. To ask earnestly: ....
3. To prevent someone from doing something: ....
4. To worsen: ....
5. To add or combine into one: ....
6. To run away secretly:..

Answers: 1-démarche; 2-urge; 3-refrain; 4-deteriorate; 5-integrate; 6-abscond.

Lesson Three

[A] Speak aloud the following words five time each

	Words	*Pronunciations*
1.	Succumb	sə'kʌm
2.	Compel	kəm'pel
3.	Indulge	ɪn'dʌldz
4.	Renew	rɪ'nju:
5.	Resolve	rɪ'zolv
6.	Abhor	əb'hɔ: (r)
7.	Aggravate	'ægrə,veɪt.

[B] Usage Practice

1. **SUCCUMB:**

- **Meaning:** To give way under pressure.
- **Sentence:** At last the criminals had to succumb before the police.
- **Your Sentence:** ....

....

2. **COMPEL:**

- **Meaning:** To force.
- **Sentence:** The pathetic condition of the poor lady compelled me to help her monitarily.
- **Your Sentence:** ....

....

3. **INDULGE:**

- **Meaning:** Yield freely to something that gives pleasure.
- **Sentence:** Don't indulge in wasteful activities. Instead, do something creative.
- **Your Sentence:** ....

....

4. **RENEW:**

- **Meaning:** To make new again; to refresh.
- **Sentence:** The vacation renewed my interest in the job.
- **Your Sentence:** ....

....

5. **RESOLVE:**

- **Meaning:** To decide firmly.
- **Sentence:** I have resolved to write a new book this year.
- **Your Sentence:** ....

....

6. **ABHOR:**

- **Meaning:** To hate strongly.
- **Sentence:** I abhor conspirators.
- **Your Sentence:** ....

....

7. **AGGRAVATE:**

- **Meaning:** To make bitter.
- **Sentence:** Sunanda's disobedience has aggravated her already hostile relations with her father.

- **Your Sentence:** ....

  ....

[C] Write the words you have learnt in this chapter in front of their meanings.

1. To give way under pressure:....................................
2. To force:..
3. To yield freely to something pleasant: ....
4. To refresh, or make new again:..................................
5. To decide firmly: ....
6. To hate strongly:...
7. To make worse: ....

Answers: 1-succumb; 2-compel; 3-indulge; 4-renew; 5-resolve; 6- abhor; 7- aggravate.

Lesson Four

[A] Speak aloud the following words five times each

Words	*Pronunciations*
1. Apprise	əˈpreɪz
2. Reiterate	ri:ˈtə,reɪt
3. Adhere	ədˈhɪə(r)
4. Harass	ˈhærəs
5. Dominate	ˈdomɪ,neɪt
6. Aspire	əˈspaɪə(r)
7. Annihilate	əˈnaɪə,leɪt

[B] Usage practice

1. **APPRISE:**
   - **Meaning:** To inform.
   - **Sentence:** The students apprised the principal about the problems they were facing in the hostel.
   - **Your Sentence:** ....

     ....

2. **REITERATE:**
   - **Meaning:** To repeat one's words or actions.
   - **Sentence:** The little girl reiterated that she had seen a thief in the house, but nobody believed her.

- **Your Sentence:** ....
  ....

3. **ADHERE:**
   - **Meaning:** To stick to or follow (the rules).
   - **Sentence:** Nobody relies on people who don't adhere to what they say.
   - **Your Sentence:** ....
     ....

4. **HARASS:**
   - **Meaning:** To annoy by troubling repeatedly.
   - **Sentence:** Many seniors love to harass the first year students.
   - **Your Sentence:** ....
     ....

5. **DOMINATE:**
   - **Meaning:** To exercise control over.
   - **Sentence:** Intelligence has enabled humans to dominate all animals.
   - **Your Sentence:** ....
     ....

6. **ASPIRE:**
   - **Meaning:** To desire for; to long for.
   - **Sentence:** Students should aspire to get the topmost rank in class.
   - **Your Sentence:** ....
     ....

7. **ANNIHILATE:**
   - **Meaning:** To destroy completely.

- **Sentence:**
  (1) The invaders[*a] annihilated the whole empire.
  (2) The raiders[*b] annihilated the village brutally.[*c]
  (3) AIDS annihilates the immune system of the body rendering it vulnerable[*d] to many other diseases.

- **Your Sentences:**
  Annihilate: ....
  Invaders: ....
  Raiders: ....
  Brutally: ....
  Vulnerable: ....

[C] Match the words in column 'A' with their meanings in column 'B'

Column A	*Column B*
1. Apprise	(a) to trouble repeatedly.
2. Reiterate	(b) too prone to be influenced or damaged.
3. Adhere	(c) inform.
4. Harass	(d) cruelly..
5. Dominate	(e) to repeat.
6. Aspire	(f) to stick to.
7. Annihilate	(g) to hope for, or desire for.
8. Brutally	(h) to exercise control over.

---

*a. Invaders are those who attack for money, valuables etc. Their attack may be quick, or very gradual.

*b. Raiders: Raiders make short-lasting, quick attacks for money or valuables.

*c. Brutally: cruelly.

*d. Vulnerable: too prone to be influenced or damaged.

9. Vulnerable (i) to destroy completely.

Answers: 1-c; 2-e; 3-f; 4-a; 5-h; 6-g; 7-i; 8-d; 9-b.

[D] Write down the words you have learnt in this chapter in front of their meanings

1. To inform: ....
2. To repeat: ....
3. To stick to: ....
4. To trouble repeatedly: ....
5. To exercise control over: ....
6. To hope for: ....
7. To destroy completely: ....
8. Cruelly: ....
9. Too prone to be damaged or influenced: ....

Answers: 1-Apprise; 2-Reiterate; 3-Adhere; 4-Harass; 5-Dominate; 6-Aspire; 7-Annihilate; 8-Brutally; 9-Vulnerable.

Lesson Five

[A] Speak aloud the following words five times each

Words	*Pronunciations*
1. Refute	rɪ'fju:t
2. Mollify	'molɪ,faɪ
3. Flay	fleɪ
4. Devastate	'devə,steɪt
5. Misconstrue	,mɪskən'stru:
6. Afflict	ə'flɪkt
7. Culminate	'kʌlmɪ,neɪt.

[B] Let us practise the usage of these words now

1. REFUTE:

- **Meaning:** To prove to be wrong or deny.
- **Sentence:** The eyewitness refuted all the statements of the criminal.
- **Your Sentence:** ....

....

2. MOLLIFY:

- **Meaning:** To pacify or lessen the severity of.
- **Sentence:** "Flattery cannot mollify your punishment," the judge told the criminal.

- **Your Sentence:** ....
  ....

3. **FLAY:**

- **Meaning**: To strip off somebody's skin [eg. by beating].

A person's biting remarks may also 'flay' a person i.e. literally, they may be severe enough to strip off the skin of someone.

- **Sentences:** The angry policeman flayed the criminal.
- Shivani flayed her husband by her acrimonious remarks.
- **Your Sentence:** ....
  ....

4. **DEVASTATE:**

- **Meaning:** To destroy on a large scale.
- **Sentence:** The raiders devastated the city within hours.
- **Your Sentence:** ....
  ....

5. **MISCONSTRUE:**

- **Meaning:** To misinterpret.
- **Sentence:** Albert misconstrued the innocent intentions of his wife.
- **Your Sentence:** ....
  ....

6. **AFFLICT:**

- **Meaning:** To make someone suffer.

- **Sentence:** Hypothyroidism afflicts a major population living in hilly areas.
- **Your Sentence:** ....

....

7. **CULMINATE:**
    - **Meaning:** To reach the highest point, or climax.
    - **Sentence:** R. L. Stevenson's fame culminated with the success of his novel 'The Treasure Island'.
    - **Your Sentence:** ....

    ....

[C] Match the following:

	Words		*Meanings*
1.	Refute	(a)	to misinterpret.
2.	Mollify	(b)	to strip off the skin.
3.	Flay	(c)	to reach the highest point.
4.	Devastate	(d)	to lessen the severity of.
5.	Misconstrue	(e)	to make someone suffer with pain or grief.
6.	Afflict	(f)	to destroy on a large scale.
7.	Culminate	(g)	to prove to be wrong.

Answers: 1-g; 2-d; 3-b; 4-f; 5-a; 6-e; 7-c.

[D] Try to recall the words you have learnt in this chapter

1. R .... (to prove to be wrong).
2. M .... (to lessen the severity of).
3. F .... (to strip off the skin).
4. D .... (to destroy).

5. M..................................... (to misinterpret).
6. A..................................... (to make someone suffer).
7. C..................................... (to reach the highest point).

Answers: 1-refute; 2-mollify; 3-flay; 4-devastate; 5-misconstrue; 6-afflict; 7-culminate.

Lesson Six

[A] Speak aloud the following words five times each.

Words	Pronunciations
1. Stifle	'staɪf(ə)l
2. Infuse	ɪn'fju:z
3. Disburse	dɪs'b3:s
4. Provoke	prə'vəʊk
5. Languish	'læŋgwɪʃ
6. Cajole	kə'dzəʊl
7. Camouflage	'kæmə,fla:z

[B] Usage practice

1 **STIFLE:**

- **Meaning:** To suppress, or suffocate.
- **Sentence:** In India, the ambitions of many girls, get stifled after their marriage.
- **Your Sentence:** ....

....

2 **INFUSE:**

- **Meaning:** Instil into.
- **Sentence:** Subhash Chandra Bose infused patriotism and courage in the Indian slaves.

- **Your Sentence:** ....

  ....

3. **DISBURSE:**
   - **Meaning:** To expend (money).
   - **Sentence:** I have disbursed all my money for buying a flat in New Delhi.
   - **Your Sentence:** ....

     ....

4. **PROVOKE:**
   - **Meaning:** To stimulate, or instigate; to goad to action.
   - **Sentence:** Rajiv Gandhi's murder provoked Indians to take revenge.
   - **Your Sentence:** ....

     ....

5. **LANGUISH:**
   - **Meaning:** To become weak.
   - **Sentence:** The woman languished in the grief of her husband's death.
   - **Your Sentence:** ....

     ....

6. **CAJOLE:**
   - **Meaning:** To persuade by flattery.
   - **Sentence:** The clerk cajoled the authorities to get a promotion.
   - **Your Sentence:** ....

     ....

7. **CAMOUFLAGE:**
   - **Meaning:** To disguise or hide something by using

natural things like plants, trees, grasses, or artificial things like wigs, fake moustaches, etc.

- **Sentence:** The detective camouflaged his identity by coloured contact lenses.
- **Your Sentence:** ....
....

[C] Match the following:

	Words		*Meaning*
1.	Stifle	(a)	to stimulate, or goad to action.
2.	Infuse	(b)	instil into.
3.	Disburse	(c)	to disguise.
4.	Provoke	(d)	to suppress.
5.	Languish	(e)	to become weak.
6.	Cajole	(f)	to diffuse or penetrate.
7.	Camouflage	(g)	to expend money.

Answers: 1-d; 2-f; 3-g; 4-a; 5-e; 6-b; 7-c.

[D] Can you recall the words you have learnt in this chapter?

1. S ....
2. I ....
3. D ....
4. P ....
5. L ....
6. C ....
7. C ....

Lesson Seven

TEST YOUR PROGRESS

First revise exercise 'B' of all the chapters covered in this assignment before taking this test. That will help you score the highest !

[A] Match the following:

	Words		*Meanings*
1.	Rejuvinate	(a)	to exemplify.
2.	Epitomise	(b)	to follow
3.	Deplete.	(c)	to ask earnestly.
4.	Ensue	(d)	to prevent from doing something.
5.	Demarche	(e)	to force.
6.	Urge	(f)	to make youthful again.
7.	Refrain	(g)	to combine into one.
8.	Integrate	(h)	to empty.
9.	Compel	(i)	to yield freely to something pleasant.
10.	Indulge	(j)	to take political steps.

[B] Fill in the blanks. You select the words from the key provided below.

1. deteriorate. 2. Succumb, 3. renew, 4. resolve, 5. reiterate, 6. adhere, 7. dominate, 8. mollify; 9. devastate, 10. stifle.

1. .... to your plans if you want to succeed! (hint: to stick to).
2. The gorgeous party has .... my energy. (Hint: to refresh).
3. The enemies had to .... in front of the Indian army. [Hint: to give way under force.]
4. Many industrialists try to .... the desires of the labourers. [Hint: to suppress or suffocate].
5. The raiders .... the entire land within hours! [Hint: to destroy on a large scale].
6. Husbands try to .... their wives, but only a few succeed. [Hint: to exercise control over].
7. On my birthday I .... to visit my daughter in London. [Hint: to decide firmly].
8. The alarming population explosion has .... the standard of living of the people. [Hint: to worsen].
9. The parents tried to .... their embittered relations with their children. [Hint: to lessen the severity of; to make smaller the proportions of to pacify].
10. The Prime Minister .... that he is doing his best to free the captives from the hijackers [Hint: to repeat].

Answers:

[A] 1-f; 2-a; 3-h; 4-b; 5-j; 6-c; 7-d; 8-g; 9-e; 10-i.

[B] 1-adhere; 2-renewed; 3-succumb; 4-stifle; 5-devastated; 6-dominate; 7-resolved; 8-deteriorated; 9-mollify; 10-reiterated.

Calculate your marks by giving +1 to each correct answer.

Marks obtained	***Remarks***
16-20	Excellent!
14-15	Very good
12-13	Good
8-1	Fair
5-7	Average
below 5	Poor

Write the remark you got in this test in the circle provided below in BOLD CAPITAL LETTERS with RED SKETCH PEN.

This is the remark our student got in this test which indicates how he/she is progressing through this course.

Words enable you to challenge the world!

ASSIGNMENT THREE. . . ADJECTIVES

Lesson One

[A] Speak aloud the following words five times each.

	Words	*Pronunciations*
1.	Valiant	ʹvæljənt
2.	Reluctant	rɪʹlʌkt(ə)nt
3.	Frail	freɪl
4.	Indefatigable	ˌɪndɪˋfætɪgəb(ə)l
5.	Immense	ɪʹmens
6.	Intractable	ɪnʹtræktəb(ə)l
7.	Ruthless	ʹru:θlɪs

[B] Usage practice

1. VALIANT:
   - **Meaning:** Brave.
   - **Sentence:** Chittor was ruled by valiant Rajput warriors.
   - **Your Sentence:** ....

     ....

2. RELUCTANT:
   - **Meaning:** Unwilling.
   - **Sentence:** Anjana was very reluctant to join the engineering profession because she had always dreamt of becoming a doctor.

- **Your Sentence:** ....

  ....

3. **FRAIL:**

- **Meaning:** Weak.
- **Sentence:** His son is the only support of the frail old man.
- **Your Sentence:** ....

  ....

4. **INDEFATIGABLE:**

- **Meaning:** One who never gets tired.
- **Sentence:** We need indefatigable youth in our army.
- **Your Sentence:** ....

  ....

5. **IMMENSE:**

- **Meaning:** Very great or huge a matter of.
- **Sentence:** Vaccination of children is of immense importance.
- **Your Sentence:** ....

  ....

6. **INTRACTABLE:**

- **Meaning: (1):** (A person) too difficult to change.
- **Sentence:** Intractable alcoholics are a nuisance—they are good for nothing.
- **Your Sentence:** ....

  ....

- **Meaning (2):** (a) disease too difficult to cure.
- **Sentence:** Many children in India suffer from intractable diarrhoea.
- **Your Sentence:** ....

  ....

- **Meaning (3):** (a problem) too difficult to solve.
- **Sentence:** Sometimes people have intractable adjustment problems in married life.
- **Your Sentence:** ....

....

7. **RUTHLESS:**

- **Meaning:** Pitiless; passionless.
- **Sentences:** Even the devil screamed on seeing the ruthless murder.
- "May God never give such a ruthless wife to any man !", the husband cried.
- **Your Sentence:** ....

....

[C] Match the following:

	Words		*Meanings*
1.	Valiant	(a)	unwilling to respond.
2.	Reluctant	(b)	huge.
3.	Frail	(c)	brave.
4.	Indefatigable	(d)	too difficult to handle.
5.	Immense	(e)	tireless.
6.	Intractable	(f)	weak.
7.	Ruthless	(g)	pitiless.

Answers: 1-c; 2-a; 3-f; 4-e; 5-b; 6-d; 7-g.

[D] Try to recall the words you have learnt in this chapter.

1. V ....
2. R..................................
3. F ....
4. I ....
5. I ....
6. I ....
7. R..................................

Lesson Two

[A] Pronounce the following words five times each

	Words	*Pronunciations*
1.	Lucrative	ˈlu:krətɪv
2.	Evasive	ɪ`veɪsɪv
3.	Luxurious	lʌgˈzjʊərɪəs
4.	Sceptical	ˈskeptɪk(ə)l
5.	Hasty	ˈheɪstɪ
6.	Mercenary	ˈmɜ:sɪnərɪ
7.	Egregious	ɪˈgri:dzəs

[B] Usage practice

1. LUCRATIVE:

- **Meaning:** Highly profitable.
- **Sentence:** Professionals have lucrative opportunities in America and Saudi Arabia.
- **Your Sentence:** ....

....

2. EVASIVE:

- **Meaning:** Not clear or direct in one's statement.
- **Sentence:** When Jack proposed to Rose for marriage, she gave him an evasive reply.

- **Your Sentence:** ....
  ....

3. **LUXURIOUS:**
   - **Meaning:** Extremely comfortable (but very costly).
   - **Sentence:** Middle class people long for a luxurious life-style.
   - **Your Sentence:** ....
     ....

4. **SCEPTICAL:**
   - **Meaning:** Too suspicious about everything; a person who questions a lot the established facts or beliefs.
   - **Sentence:** It is very difficult to tolerate a sceptical wife.
   - **Your Sentence:** ....
     ....

5. **HASTY:**
   - **Meaning:** In a hurry.
   - **Sentence:** Hasty decisions frequently result in blunders.
   - **Your Sentence:** ....
     ....

6. **MERCENARY:**
   - **Meaning:** A very greedy person, who does any work only for the sake of profit or reward.
   - **Sentence:** In todays materialistic world, you will find mercenary people everywhere !
   - **Your Sentence:** ....
     ....

7. **EGREGIOUS:**

- **Meaning:** Worst; bad beyond comparison.
- **Sentence:** Let us all take a pledge to eradicate the egregious dowry system.
- **Your Sentence:** ....

....

[C] Match the following:

Words		*Meanings*
1. Lucrative	(a)	extremely comfortable, but costly.
2. Evasive	(b)	One who works only for the sake of profit or award.
3. Luxurious	(c)	hurried.
4. Sceptical	(d)	not clear or direct in one's answer or statement.
5. Hasty	(e)	too bad.
6. Mercenary	(f)	highly profitable.
7. Egregious	(g)	too suspicious about everything.

Answers: 1-f; 2-d; 3-a; 4-g; 5-c; 6-b; 7-e.

[D] Try to recall the words you have learnt in this chapter.

1. .... : highly profitable.
2. .... : not clear or direct in one's statements.
3. .... : Extremely comfortable, but costly.
4. .... : Suspicious.
5. .... : hurried.
6. .... : a greedy person, who works only for the sake of money or reward.

7. .... : very bad.

Answers: 1-lucrative; 2-evasive; 3-luxurious; 4-sceptical; 5-hasty; 6-mercenary; 7-egregious.

Lesson Three

[A] Pronounce the following words five times each

	Words	***Pronunciations***
1.	Ethnic	'eθnɪk
2.	Multifarious	,mʌltɪ'feərɪəs
3.	Gigantic	dzaɪ'gæntɪk
4.	Unprecedented	ʌn'presɪ,dentɪd
5.	Enigmatic	,enɪg'mætɪk
6.	Iconoclastic	aɪ,konə'klæstɪk
7.	Fastidious	fæ'stɪdɪəs

[B] Usage practice

1. ETHNIC:

- **Meaning:** Belonging to a social group having a common culture and traditions.
- **Sentence:** It is very interesting to interact with people of diverse ethnic groups in India.
- **Your Sentence:** ....

....

2. MULTIFARIOUS:

- **Meaning:** Of various types; many.
- **Sentence:** Multifarious opportunities knock the doors of hard-working students.

- **Your Sentence:** ....

  ....

3. **GIGANTIC:**

- **Meaning:** Of huge size; colossal.
- **Sentence:** The gigantic Statue of Liberty filled me with awe and admiration.
- **Your Sentence:** ....

  ....

4. **UNPRECEDENTED:**

- **Meaning:** Unparalleled; having no comparison.
- **Sentence:** Whole world was fascinated by the unprecedented acting of Goldie Hawn, the actress.
- **Your Sentence:** ....

  ....

5. **ENIGMATIC:**

- **Meaning:** Puzzling; like a riddle.
- **Sentence:** Everybody was shocked by the enigmatic disappearance of the prisoner.
- **Your Sentence:** ....

  ....

6. **ICONOCLASTIC:**

- **Meaning:** This word has been derived from 'icon' and 'clast'. Icon means an idol or image, and clast means 'to break'. Iconoclast, or an iconoclastic person, is one who breaks or attacks established 'images' or ideas. So, ICONOCLASTIC means one who attacks or breaks established beliefs or principles.
- **Sentence:** The iconoclastic remarks of the social worker stunned the society.
- **Your Sentence:** ....

  ....

7. FASTIDIOUS:

- **Meaning:** A fussy person who tries to find out too many details. Such a person is unhappy about everything. He easily gets irritated and annoyed. [Would you like to have a fastidious life partner?]
- **Sentence:** A fastidious life partner is a virtual devil on earth.
- **Your Sentence:** ....

[C] Match the following:

	Words		*Meanings*
1.	Ethnic	(a).	Of various kinds.
2.	Multifarious	(b)	A social group having a common culture and tradition.
3.	Gigantic	(c)	unparalleled.
4.	Unprecedented	(d)	One who breaks established beliefs or principles.
5.	Enigmatic	(e)	huge.
6.	Iconoclastic	(f)	too inquisitive about details.
7.	Fastidious	(g)	puzzling.

Answers: 1-b; 2-a; 3-e; 4-c; 5-g; 6-d; 7-f.

[D] Try to recall the words you have learnt in this chapter

1. E ....
2. M ....
3. G ....
4. U ....
5. E ....
6. I ....
7. F ....

Lesson Four

[A] Pronounce the following words five times each

	Words	***Pronunciations***
1.	Scintillating	'sɪntɪ,leɪtɪŋ
2.	Industrious	in'dʌstrɪəs
3.	Murky	'mɜ:kɪ
4.	Lucid	'lu:sɪd
5.	Poignant	'pɔinjənt
6.	Jubilant	'dzu:bilənt
7.	Formidable	'fɔ:mɪdəb(ə)l

[B] Usage Practice

1. SCINTILLATING:

- **Meaning:** Shining brightly; sparkling; brilliant (in career etc.).
- **Sentence:** Sachin Tendulkar's scintillating performance in the cricket match stupefied the whole world!
- **Your Sentence:** ....

  ....

2. INDUSTRIOUS:

- **Meaning:** Hard working.
- **Sentence:** Only the industrious students can get admission in the Oxford University.
- **Your Sentence:** ....

  ....

3. **MURKY:**

- **Meaning (1):** Dark.
- **Sentence:** Even the tough hunters fear the murky forests of Satpura.
- **Your Sentence:** ....

....

- **Meaning (2):** Sad, down in spirits, or gloomy.
- **Sentence:** The widow is trying to come out of her murky past.
- **Your Sentence:** ....

....

4. **LUCID:**

- **Meaning:** Clear, obvious; easy to understand.
- **Sentence:** Enid Blyton knew that children love reading lucid stories.
- **Your Sentence:** ....

....

5. **POIGNANT:**

- **Meaning:** Piercing: [even words may be as piercing as a needle sufficient to wound a person emotionally].
- **Sentence:** Tears rolled down her eyes on hearing her husbands poignant remarks.
- **Your Sentence:** ....

....

6. **JUBILANT:**

- **Meaning:** Cheerful.
- **Sentence:**
- **Your sentence:** ....

....

7. FORMIDABLE:

- **Meaning:** Fearful.
- **Sentence: (1):** Nobody ever spent a night in the formidable guest house," the villager told us.

  (2) Many girls hate the formidable problems of Mathematics.
- **Your Sentence:** ....

  ....

[C] Match the following:

	Words		*Meanings*
1.	Scintillating	(a)	hard working
2.	Industrious	(b)	dark
3.	Murky	(c)	sparkling
4.	Lucid	(d)	piercing
5.	Poignant	(e)	fearful
6.	Jubilant	(f)	clear
7.	Formidable	(g)	cheerful

Answers: 1-c; 2-a; 3-b; 4-f; 5-d; 6-g; 7-e.

[D] Can you spell the words correctly? Let us test you for spellings now. Write down the words you have learnt in this chapter in the blanks provided below.

1. .... : Shining brightly
2. .... : Hard-working
3. .... : Gloomy; dark.
4. .... : Clear
5. .... : Piercing
6. .... : Cheerful
7. .... : Dreadful; fearful.

Answers: 1-scintillating: 2-industrious; 3-murky; 4-lucid; 5-poignant; 6- jubilant 7-formidable.

Lesson Five

[A] Speak aloud the following words five times each.

	Words	*Pronunciations*
1.	Eloquent	'eləkwənt
2.	Hideous	'hɪdɪəs
3.	Cannibalistic	,kænɪbə'lɪstɪk
4.	Remote	rɪməʊt
5.	Gorgeous	'gɔ:dzəs
6.	Dubious	'dju:bɪəs
7.	Undaunted	ʌn'dɔntɪd

[B] Usage practice

1. ELOQUENT:

- **Meaning:** Fluent and clear (speech).
- **Sentence:** The college president gave an eloquent speech on winning the elections.
- **Your Sentence:** ....

....

2. HIDEOUS:

- **Meaning:** Repulsive; ugly.
- **Sentence:** (1) Their poverty has forced them to live in the hideous slum areas.

  (2) The whole world detested the hideous crime.

- **Your Sentence:** ....

  ....

3. **CANNIBALISTIC:**

- **Meaning:** One who eats others of his own kind eg. a human who eats human flesh.
- **Sentence:** Hunger forced the men trapped in the tunnel to become cannibalistic.
- **Your Sentence:** ....

  ....

4. **REMOTE:**

- **Meaning:** Distant; far off
- **Sentence:** It is very difficult to provide efficient health services in the remote rural areas.
- **Your Sentence:** ....

  ....

5. **GORGEOUS:**

- **Meaning:** Splendid; marvellous; outstanding.
- **Sentence:** Have you ever seen the gorgeous Niagra waterfalls?
- **Your Sentence:** ....

  ....

6. **DUBIOUS:**

- **Meaning:** Doubtful.
- **Sentence:** "Her chances of survival are dubious," the doctor revealed.
- **Your Sentence:** ....

  ....

7. UNDAUNTED:

- **Meaning:** One who cannot be frightened.
- **Sentence:** The undaunted warriors decapitated the enemy soldiers. (decapitate: to cut the head off).
- **Your Sentence:** ....
....

[C] Match the following:

	Words		*Meanings*
1.	Eloquent	(a)	One who cannot be frightened.
2.	Hideous	(b)	distant
3.	Cannibalistic	(c)	doubtful
4.	Remote	(d)	One who eats others of his own kind.
5.	Gorgeous	(e)	fluent, clear and impressive
6.	Dubious	(f)	wonderful; splendid.
7.	Undaunted.	(g)	Ugly and repulsive.

Answers: 1-e; 2-g; 3-d; 4-b; 5-f; 6-c; 7-a.

[D] Try to recall the words you have learnt in this chapter.

1. E ....
2. H ....
3. C ....
4. R ....
5. G ....
6. D ....
7. U ....

Lesson Six

[A] Pronunciation practice

Speak aloud the following words five times each

	Words	*Pronunciations*
1.	Alien	ʹeɪlɪən
2.	Wary	ʹweərɪ
3.	Clandestine	klænʹdestɪn
4.	Imperative	ɪmʹperətɪv
5.	Punitive	ʹpju:nɪtɪv
6.	Authentic	ɔ: ʹθentɪk
7.	Bellicose	ʹbelɪ,kəʊz

[B] Usage practice

1. ALIEN:

- **Meaning:** Foreign.
- **Sentence:** I would love to visit the alien world.
- **Your Sentence:** ....

....

2. WARY:

- **Meaning:** Alert; cautious and watchful.
- **Sentence:** The wary guard caught the thief red-handed.

- **Your Sentence:** ....

  ....

3. **CLANDESTINE:**

- **Meaning:** Secret.
- **Sentence:** Jack and Rose had many clandestine meetings on the ship 'Titanic'.
- **Your Sentence:** ....

  ....

4. **IMPERATIVE:**

- **Meaning:** Necessary.
- **Sentence:** Dialysis is imperative for the health of kidney failure patients.
- **Your Sentence:** ....

  ....

5. **PUNITIVE:**

- **Meaning:** Infliting punishment, retributive
- **Sentence:** Every student was afraid of the punitive teacher.
- **Your Sentence:** ....

  ....

6. **AUTHENTIC:**

- **Meaning:** Genuine; true.
- **Sentence:** The jewellery Alice was flaunting in the party was not authentic.
- **Your Sentence:** ....

  ....

7. BELLICOSE:

- **Meaning:** War-loving; aggressive; revolting.
- **Sentence:** Many bellicose tribes live in the equatorial forests.
- **Your Sentence:** ....
....

[C] Match the following:

	Words		*Meanings*
1.	Alien	(a)	necessary
2.	Wary	(b)	one who loves giving punishment.
3.	Clandestine	(c)	war-loving
4.	Imperative	(d)	alert
5.	Punitive	(e)	strange; foreign.
6.	Authentic	(f)	secret
7.	Bellicose	(g)	genuine.

Answers: 1-e; 2-d; 3-f; 4-a; 5-b; 6-g; 7-c.

[D] Write down the words you have learnt in this chapter in front of their meanings.

1. Foreign: ....
2. Alert: ....
3. Secret: ....
4. Necessary: ....
5. One who loves giving punishment: ....
6. Genuine: ....
7. War-loving: ....

Answers: 1-alien; 2-wary; 3-clandestine; 4-imperative; 5-punitive; 6-authentic; 7-bellicose.

Lesson Seven

TEST YOUR PROGRESS

Revise exercise 'B' of all the chapters discussed in this assignment before taking this test. You already know by now, that revision helps you score higher.

[A] Match the following:

	Words		*Meanings*
1.	Valiant	(a)	highly profitable
2.	Reluctant	(b)	of various kinds
3.	Lucrative	(c)	huge
4.	Evasive	(d)	brave
5.	Multifarious	(e)	hard-working
6.	Gigantic	(f)	fluent and clear
7.	Industrious	(g)	unwilling
8.	Murky	(h)	ugly and repulsive
9.	Eloquent	(i)	not clear (in one's statements)
10.	Hideous	(j)	dark; gloomy.

[B] Match the following:

	Words		*Meaning*
1.	Frail	(a)	piercing
2.	Indefatigable	(b)	weak
3.	Luxurious	(c)	Clear

4. Sceptical (d) tireless

5. Enigmatic (e) one who eats others of his own kind

6. Lucid (f) splendid; wonderful.

7. Poignant (g) very comfortable, but costly

8. Cannibalistic (h) one who loves giving punishment

9. Gorgeous (i) suspicious

10. Punitive (j) puzzling.

Answers:

[A] 1-d; 2-g; 3-a; 4-i; 5-b; 6-c; 7-e; 8-j; 9-f; 10-h;

[B] 1-b; 2-d; 3-g; 4-i; 5-j; 6-c; 7-a; 8-e; 9-f; 10-h.

Your Score: Give yourself +1 marks for each correct answer. Add up your marks to get your score.

Marks obtained	***Remarks***
18-20	Excellent
15-17	Very good
12-14	Good
8-11	Fair
5-7	Average
Below 5	Poor

Write the remark you got in this test in the circle provided below in BOLD, CAPITAL LETTERS, with RED SKETCH PEN.

This is the remark our student got in this test which indicates how he/she is progressing through this course.

PART TWO

Good vocabulary enables you to communicate effectively . . .

Assignment Four. . . Nouns

Lesson One

[A] Speak aloud the following words five times each.

	Words	***Pronunciations***
1.	Cliché	'kli:ʃeɪ
2.	Plea	pli:
3.	Allegation	'ælɪgeiʃ(ə)n
4.	Coincidence	kəʊ'ɪnsɪd(ə)ns
5.	Blitz	blɪts
6.	Contrary	'KontrərI
7.	Havoc	'hævək
8.	Subterfuge	's^btə,fju:dz
9.	Fortitude	'fɔ:tɪ,tju:d

[B] Usage practice:

1. CLICHE:

- **Meaning:** Cliché is something (like a joke, idea, etc.) which has become stale due to overuse or repetition. It lacks originality basically, and is quite uninteresting.
- **Sentence:** The movie is nothing but a collection of clichés.
- **Your Sentence:** ....

  ....

2. **PLEA:**

   - **Meaning:** An earnest appeal.
   - **Sentence:** Even God doesn't hear the plea of a lazy man!
   - **Your Sentence:** ....

     ....

3. **ALLEGATION:**

   - **Meaning:** A forceful declaration (especially of something which lacks proof).
   - **Sentence:** The allegation, that Kapil Dev is involved in match-fixing, shocked the whole world.
   - **Your Sentence:** ....

     ....

4. **COINCIDENCE:**

   - **Meaning:** The simultaneous occurrence of apparently connected incidents.
   - **Sentence:** By coincidence, my friend Sheeba and I, got a seat in the same medical college.
   - **Your Sentence:** ....

     ....

5. **BLITZ:**

   - **Meaning**: 'Blitz' is an abbreviation of 'blitzkrieg' which is German in origin. 'Blitzkrieg' or 'blitz' is a swift, sudden and intensive attack (at lightening speed), especially through air.
   - **Sentence:** The blitz under the leadership of American forces startled the enemies.
   - **Your Sentence:** ....

     ....

6. **CONTRARY:**

- **Meaning:** Opposite.
- **Sentence:** Contrary to the common belief, kidney failure patients have good chances of survival provided they take regular treatment.
- **Your Sentence:** ....

....

7. **HAVOC:**

- **Meaning:** Widespread destruction.
- **Sentence:** Nuclear war can result in a havoc on earth.
- **Your Sentence:** ....

....

8. **SUBTERFUGE:**

- **Meaning:** An attempt to escape something (like accusation, punishment, defeat etc.) by using a deceitful trick.
- **Sentence:** Kapil Dev's desperate subterfuges to escape the accusation were rendered futile [futile means useless].
- **Your Sentence:** ....

....

9. **FORTITUDE:**

- **Meaning:** Courage shown in difficult times.
- **Sentence:** Rana Pratap, the great warrior, is admired for his valour and fortitude.
- **Your Sentence:** ....

....

[C] Match the following:-

	Words		*Meanings*
1.	Cliche	(a)	A sudden, intensive and swift attack.
2.	Plea	(b)	Simultaneous occurrence of apparently connected events.
3.	Allegation	(c)	Widespread destruction.
4.	Coincidence	(d)	Courage in difficulties.
5.	Blitz	(e)	an attempt to escape something undesirable by deceitful tricks.
6.	Contrary	(f)	Something which has become stale due to overuse.
7.	Havoc	(g)	opposite.
8.	Subterfuge	(h)	An earnest appeal
9.	Fortitude	(i)	A forceful declaration (of something which lacks proof).

Answers: 1-f; 2-h; 3-i; 4-b; 5-a; 6-g; 7-c; 8-e; 9-d.

[D] Write the words you have learnt in this chapter in front of their meanings.

1. An idea, manner, etc. which has become stale or unattractive because of overuse: ....
2. An earnest appeal:..
3. A forceful declaration:..
4. Simultaneous occurrence of apparently connected incidents: ....
5. A sudden, swift and surprising attack:....................
6. Opposite:..
7. Widespread destruction:...

8. An attempt to escape punishment by deceitful tricks: ....

9. Courage shown in difficulties: ....

Answers: 1-cliché; 2-plea; 3-allegation; 4-coincidence; 5-blitz; 6-contrary; 7-havoc; 8-subterfuge; 9-fortitude.

Lesson Two

[A] Speak aloud the following words five times each

	Words	*Pronunciations*
1.	Turpitude	ʹtə:pɪ,tju:d
2.	Consequence	ʹkonsɪ, kwəns
3.	Coalition	,kəʊəʹlɪʃ(ə)n
4.	Nuke	nju:k
5.	Resentment	rɪʹzentmənt
6.	Fait accompli	,feɪt əʹkompli:
7.	Feud	fju:d
8.	Fomentation	,fəʊmenʹteɪʃ(ə)n
9.	Passion	ʹpæʃ(ə)n

[B] Usage practice

1. TURPITUDE

- **Meaning:** Baseness; lowliness.
- **Sentence:** I abhor the turpitude of criminals.
- **Your Sentence:** ....

  ....

2. CONSEQUENCE:

- **Meaning:** Result.
- **Sentence:** We have to bear the consequences of everything we do.

- **Your Sentence:** ....

  ....

3. **COALITION:**

- **Meaning:** Fusion.
- **Sentence:** The coalition of the two political parties has given them better stability.
- **Your Sentence:** ....

  ....

4. **NUKE:**

- **Meaning:** Nuclear weapon.
- **Sentence:** Nuke power can be misused
- **Your Sentence:** ....

  ....

5. **RESENTMENT:**

- **Meaning:** Strong and bitter anger.
- **Sentence:** C. Deepa expressed her resentment over the indecent remarks published in the magazine.
- **Your Sentence:** ....

  ....

6. ***Fait accompli:***

- **Meaning:** Something already done, which cannot be changed by any means.
- **Sentence:** "My defeat is a *fait accompli,* and I have to accept it anyway, "the old man sighed.
- **Your Sentence:** ....

  ....

7. **FEUD:**

- **Meaning:** A deadly, long-lasting dispute (between two families, groups, etc.).

- **Sentence:** The feud between Kauravas and Pandavas resulted in terrible bloodshed.
- **Your Sentence:** ....

....

8. FOMENTATION:

- **Meaning:** Application of warm, soothing fluid, or a medicated solution, to relieve pain or suffering.
- **Sentence:** "Hot water fomentations should give you relief", the doctor said.
- **Your Sentence:** ....

....

9. PASSION:

- **Meaning:** A strong, uncontrollable feeling.
- **Sentence:** My girl has a passion for flowers.
- **Your Sentence:** ....

....

[C] Match the following:

Words		*Meanings*
1. Turpitude	(a)	a strong, irresistible emotion.
2. Consequence	(b)	lowliness.
3. Coalition	(c)	something already done which cannot be altered.
4. Nuke	(d)	bitter anger
5. Resentment	(e)	application of warm, or medicated solution.
6. *Fait accompli*	(f)	result
7. Feud	(g)	long-standing, bitter deadly dispute.

8. Fomentation (h) fusion,
9. Passion (i) nuclear weapon.

Answers: 1-b; 2-f; 3-h; 4-i; 5-d; 6-c; 7-g; 8-e; 9-a.

[D] Write the words you have learnt in this chapter in front of their meanings.

1. Lowliness: ....
2. Something already done, and nothing can change it anyhow: ....
3. Fusion: ....
4. Nuclear weapon: ....
5. Bitter anger: ....
6. Result: ....
7. A strong, irresistible emotion: ....
8. A long standing, deadly dispute: ....
9. Application of warm, soothing, or medicated fluid to relieve pain or suffering: ....

Answers: 1-turpitude; 2-*fait accompli*; 3-coalition; 4-nuke; 5-resentment; 6-consequence; 7-passion; 8-feud; 9-fomentation.

Lesson Three

[A] Speak aloud the following words five times each

	Words	*Pronunciations*
1.	Impact	ˈɪmpækt
2.	Penury	ˈpenjʊrɪ
3.	Hoax	həuks
4.	Dirge	dz:dz
5.	Lust	lʌst
6.	Melodrama	ˈmelə,dra:mə
7.	Bathos	ˈbeɪθos
8.	Levity	ˈlevɪtɪ

[B] Usage practice

1. IMPACT:

- **Meaning:** A forceful collision; a strong effect.
- **Sentence:** The family atmosphere makes tremendous impact on the development of children.
- **Your Sentence:** ....

....

2. PENURY:

- **Meaning:** Poverty.
- **Sentence:** The untouchables had to live a life of penury and woe in the past.

[Woe-grief; distress].

3. **HOAX:**

- **Meaning:** A deceitful joke.
- **Sentence:** The news of his father's death turned out to be a hoax.
- **Your Sentence:** ....

4. **DIRGE:**

- **Meaning:** Dirge is a mournful song sung for the dead ones at the time of funeral. Commonly this word is used to describe a mournful lament for the past or for someone beloved who has gone away.
- **Sentence:** The widow's dirge for her good old days was pathetic.
- **Your Sentence:** ....

5. **LUST:**

- **Meaning:** Strong desire (or hunger) for (money, power, sex, etc.)
- **Sentence:** The Indian rulers had a lust for gold.
- **Your Sentence:** ....

6. **MELODRAMA:**

- **Meaning:** A sensational drama meant to excite emotions, usually having a happy end. Melodramas are only for stirring up the feelings—they have no strong substance or story.
- **Sentence:** These days producers prefer making melodramas for television, as they are highly successful.

- **Your Sentence:** ....

....

7. BATHOS:

- **Meaning:** A decline from an elevated to an ordinary level. e.g. decline from climax to an absurd end in a movie.
- **Sentence:** The ghost story 'secret of the haunted castle' broadcasted on television, is an excellent piece of bathos.
- **Your Sentence:** ....

....

8. LEVITY:

- **Meaning:** Frivolity; lack of seriousness; tendency to treat even serious matters lightly.
- **Sentence:** We were astonished to see the levity of the dying soldier.
- **Your Sentence:** ....

....

[C] Match the following:

Words	***Meanings***
1. Impact	(a) Poverty.
2. Penury	(b) Decline from an elevated to a base level.
3. Hoax	(c) A powerful effect
4. Dirge	(d) A deceitful joke.
5. Lust	(e) Lack of seriousness
6. Melodrama	(f) Mournful lament
7. Bathos	(g) Very strong desire or hunger (for money gold, etc.)

8. Levity (h) A sensational drama full of emotions, usually having a happy end.

Answers: 1-c; 2-a; 3-d; 4-f; 5-g; 6-h; 7-b; 8-e.

[D] Try to recall the words you have learnt in this chapter.

1. I ....: a strong effect.
2. P ....: poverty.
3. H ....: a deceitful joke.
4. D ....: mournful lament.
5. L ....: strong desire or hunger.
6. M ....: sensational and emotional drama.
7. L ....: lack of seriousness.

Answers: 1-impact; 2-penury; 3-hoax; 4-dirge; 5-lust; 6-melodrama; 7-levity.

Lesson Four

[A] Speak aloud the following words five time each.

	Words	*Pronunciations*
1.	Verdict	'vɜ:dɪkt
2.	Dread	dred
3.	Prosecution	'prosɪ'kju:ʃ(ə)n
4.	Testimony	'testɪmənɪ
5.	Malady	'mælədɪ
6.	Threshold	'θreʃəʊld
7.	Notion	'nəʊʃ(ə)n
8.	Endeavour	ɪn'devə(r)

[B] Usage practice:

1. VERDICT:

- **Meaning:** Decision; judgement.
- **Sentence:** (1) The prisoner is eagerly awaiting the verdict of the Supreme Court.

  (2) Think twice before giving your verdict.
- **Your Sentence:** ....

  ....

2. DREAD:

- **Meaning:** Intense fear.

- **Sentence:** The dread of AIDS has forced many people to take necessary precautions.
- **Your Sentence:** ....

....

3. **PROSECUTION:**

- **Meaning:** The legal proceedings (against a criminal).
- **Sentence:** The prosecution against the assassin concluded yesterday.
- **Your Sentence:** ....

....

4. **TESTIMONY:**

- **Meaning:** A true statement; evidence given under oath.
- **Sentence:** Let us not forget the old testimony—'God helps those who help themselves.'
- **Your Sentence:** ....

....

5. **MALADY:**

- **Meaning:** Disease.
- **Sentence:** AIDS is the dreadful malady which has no cure.
- **Your Sentence:** ....

....

6. **THRESHOLD:**

- **Meaning:** Starting point; a point at which a stimulus produces a response.
- **Sentence:** 1. India is now standing on the threshold of an economic revolution.

2. Stimuli weaker than the threshold value don't produce any response in a muscle fibre.

- **Your Sentence:** ....

....

7. **NOTION:**

- **Meaning:** Idea, opinion.
- **Sentence:** For long, I cherished the false notion that the girl loved me.
- **Your Sentence:** ....

....

8. **ENDEAVOUR:**

- **Meaning:** Effort.
- **Sentence:** The world will always remember the humanitarian endeavours of our beloved Mother Teresa.
- **Your Sentence:** ....

....

[C] Match the following:

	Words		*Meanings*
1.	Verdict	(a)	an idea
2.	Dread	(b)	effort
3.	Prosecution	(c)	disease
4.	Testimony	(d)	intense fear
5.	Malady	(e)	starting point
6.	Threshold.	(f)	a true statement under oath.
7.	Notion	(g)	judgement
8.	Endeavour	(h)	the legal proceedings (against a criminal).

Answers: 1-g; 2-d; 3-h; 4-f; 5-c; 6-e; 7-a; 8-b.

[D] Write down the words you have learnt in this chapter in front of their meanings.

1. Judgement: ....
2. Intense fear: ....
3. Legal proceedings against a criminal: ....
4. A true and testified statement: ....
5. Disease: ....
6. A starting point: ....
7. An idea or opinion: ....
8. Effort: ....

Answers: 1-verdict; 2-dread; 3-prosecution; 4-testimony; 5-malady; 6-threshold; 7-notion; 8-endeavour.

Lesson Five

[A] Pronounce the following words five times each.

	Words	*Pronunciations*
1.	Clamp-down	klæmp-daʊn
2.	Assault	ə'sɔ:lt
3.	Allusion	ə'lju:z(ə)n
4.	Bout	baʊt
5.	Anonymity	,ænə'nɪmɪtɪ
6.	Access	'ækses
7.	Elite	eɪ'li:t

[B] Usage Practice

1. CLAMP-DOWN:
   - **Meaning:** Severe restriction.
   - **Sentence:** The imprisonment put a clamp-down on the evil intentions of the criminal.
   - **Your Sentence:** ....

     ....

2. ASSAULT:
   - **Meaning:** Attack.
   - **Sentence:** Pakistan's assault on India was rendered futile by the vigilant Indian army.
   - **Your Sentence:** ....

     ....

3. **ALLUSION:**
   - **Meaning:** An indirect or passing reference.
   - **Sentence:** Rashmi wrote a very good essay on 'the Indian women' by taking numerous allusions from different books.
   - **Your Sentence:** ....
     ....

4. **BOUT:**
   - **Meaning:** A limited period (of activity, illness, exercise, etc.).
   - **Sentence:** Countless bouts of severe pain forced the cancer patient plead for death.
   - **Your Sentence:** ....
     ....

5. **ANONYMITY:**
   - **Meaning:** Namelessness.
   - **Sentence:** The informant demanded anonymity before telling the secret hiding place of the criminals.
   - **Your Sentence:** ....
     ....

6. **ACCESS**
   - **Meaning:** Point of entrance.
   - **Sentence:** It is very difficult to gain access to the chambers of high officials.
   - **Your Sentence:** ....
     ....

7. **ELITE**
   - **Meaning:** One gifted with riches and luxuries.

- **Sentence:** Middle class people tend to imitate the life-style of the elites.
- **Your Sentence:** ....
....

[C] Match the following:

	Words		*Meanings*
1.	Clamp-down	(a)	namelessness
2.	Assault	(b)	severe restriction
3.	Allusion	(c)	a period of (activity, madness)
4.	Bout	(d)	a person gifted with riches and luxuries.
5.	Anonymity	(e)	attack
6.	Access	(f)	a passing or indirect reference
7.	Elite	(g)	an entrance.

Answers: 1-b; 2-e; 3-f; 4-c; 5-a; 6-g; 7-d.

[D] Write down the words you have learnt in this chapter in front of their meanings.

1. Severe restriction: ....
2. Attack: ....
3. A passing or indirect reference: ....
4. A period of (activity, work, exercise, etc.): ....
5. Namelessness: ....
6. Entrance: ....
7. A rich man belonging to the highest gifted with a luxurious life-style: ....

Answers: 1-clamp-down; 2- assault; 3-allusion; 4-bout; 5-anonynity; 6-access; 7-elite.

Lesson Six

[A] Pronounce the following words five times each.

	Words	***Pronunciations***
1.	Ailment	ʹeɪlmənt
2.	Crisis	ʹkraɪsɪs
3.	Perception	pəʹsepʃ(ə)n
4.	Dilemma	daɪʹlemə
5.	Prospect	ʹprospekt
6.	Strategy	ʹstrætɪdʒɪ
7.	Combat	ʹkombæt
8.	Despondency	dɪʹspond(ə)nsɪ
9.	Xenomania	ˌzenəʹmænɪə

[B] Usage Practice

1. AILMENT:

- **Meaning:** A minor disease or illness.
- **Sentence:** Health ailments need proper medical care.
- **Your Sentence:** ....
  ....

2. CRISIS:

- **Meaning:** A crucial time; time of acute difficulty and danger.

- **Sentence:** Economic crisis ruined the Reema finance company.
- **Your Sentence:** ....
....

3. **PERCEPTION:**
   - **Meaning:** Intuitive understanding of (truth, solution, etc.).
   - **Sentence:** Perception of truth makes a man mature.
   - **Your Sentence:** ....
   ....

4. **DILEMMA:**
   - **Meaning:** A difficult situation, when a person is forced to choose between two equally hateful alternatives.
   - **Sentence:** I was trapped in a dilemma when my parents started forcing me to chose one of the two ugly girls for marriage.
   - **Your Sentence:** ....
   ....

5. **PROSPECT:**
   - **Meaning:** Hope (especially of success in a venture).
   - **Sentence:** Bright prospects of medical profession attract a lot of students to choose this line.
   - **Your Sentence:** ....
   ....

6. **STRATEGY:**
   - **Meaning:** Plan of action.
   - **Sentence:** The commander thought of a very good strategy to crush the enemy troops.

- **Your Sentence:** ....
  ....

7. **COMBAT:**
   - **Meaning:** Fight.
   - **Sentence:** The deadly combat between the two warriors ended in their death.
   - **Your Sentence:** ....
     ....

8. **DESPONDENCY**
   - **Meaning:** Sadness : gloom
   - **Sentence:** "Never let despondency rule thy heart, baby," the mother said.
   - **Your Sentence:** ....
     ....

9. **XENOMANIA:**
   - **Meaning:** Too much attraction (to the extent of madness) for foreign objects, or foreigners.
   - **Sentence:** Xenomania is widespread among people of developing countries.
   - **Your Sentence:** ....
     ....

[C] Match the following:

	Words		*Meanings*
1.	Ailment	(a)	a crucial period.
2.	Crisis	(b)	hope.
3.	Perception	(c)	fight.
4.	Dilemma	(d)	illness, especially a minor one.
5.	Prospect	(e)	sadness.
6.	Strategy	(f)	a difficult situation, when a

			person is forced to choose between two equally disagreeable alternatives.
7.	Combat	(g)	a plan of action.
8.	Despondency	(h)	intuitive understanding.
9.	Xenomania	(i)	excessive attraction for foreign objects or foreigners.

Answers: 1-d; 2-a; 3-h; 4-f; 5-b; 6-g; 7-c; 8-e; 9-i.

[D] Try to recall the words, you have learnt in this chapter.

1. A ....
2. C ....
3. P ....
4. D ....
5. P ....
6. S ....
7. C ....
8. D ....
9. X ....

Lesson Seven

TEST YOUR PROGRESS

Revise exercise 'B' of all the chapters discussed in this assignment before taking this test.

[A] Match the following:

Words		*Meanings*
1. Havoc	(a)	a mournful lamentation.
2. Penury	(b)	severe restriction.
3. Dirge	(c)	a passing reference.
4. Notion	(d)	a time of difficulties; a crucial time.
5. Malady	(e)	an idea
6. Testimony	(f)	a true and testified statement.
7. Clamp-down	(g)	widespread destruction.
8. Allusion	(h)	fight.
9. Crisis	(i)	disease
10. Combat	(j)	poverty.

[B] Match the following:

Words		*Meanings*
1. *fait-accompli*	(a)	a situation in which one has to choose between two equally hateful options.

2. Nuke	(b) expectation.
3. Hoax	(c) starting point.
4. Threshold	(d) an unchangeable result.
5. Verdict	(e) a nuclear weapon.
6. Assault	(f) sadness.
7. Anonymity	(g) judgement.
8. Dilemma	(h) namelessness.
9. Prospect	(i) attack.
10. Despondency	(j) a deceitful joke.

Answers: [A] 1-g; 2-j; 3-a; 4-e; 5-i; 6-f; 7-b; 8-c; 9-d; 10-h.

[B] 1-d; 2-e; 3-j; 4-c; 5-g; 6-i; 7-h; 8-a; 9-b; 10-f.

Your marks: Give yourself +1 for every correct answer, and calculate your total marks.

Marks obtained	***Remarks***
18-20	Excellent
15-17	Very good
12-14	Good
8-11	Fair
5-7	Average
Below 5	Poor.

Write down the remarks you got in this test in the space provided below in BOLD CAPITAL LETTERS, with RED SKETCH PEN.

This is the remark our student got in this test which indicates how he/she is progressing through this course.

Good words impress anyone!

Assignment Five. . . Verbs

Lesson One

[A] Speak aloud the following words five times each

	Words	*Pronunciations*
1.	Foist	fɔɪst
2.	Whittle	ʼwɪt (ə)l
3.	Assault	əʼsɔ:lt
4.	Connote	kəʼnəʊt
5.	Dwindle	ʼdwɪnd (ə)l
6.	Daunt	dɔ:nt
7.	Contaminate	kənʼtæmɪ,neɪt

[B] Usage practice

1. FOIST:

- **Meaning:** Try to force someone to accept a fake object, or something ordinary (by making him believe that it is genuine or very valuable).
- **Sentence:** The shopkeeper tried to foist on me a defective transistor.
- **Your Sentence:** ....

  ....

2. WHITTLE:

- **Meaning:** To reduce the size of something by slicing it off repeatedly.

- **Sentence:** The butcher whittled away the mutton piece within no time.
- "Multiple failures have whittled down my self confidence," the boy replied.
- **Your Sentence:** ....

....

3. **ASSAULT:**

- **Meaning:** To attack.
- **Sentence:** The Indian troops assaulted the enemies in the dark night.
- **Your Sentence:** ....

....

4. **CONNOTE:**

- **Meaning:** To mean, or denote.
- **Sentence:** Your negligence connotes your lack of interest in the job.
- **Your Sentence:** ....

....

5. **DWINDLE:**

- **Meaning:** To reduce (in size, number, or importance).
- **Sentence:** The chief's importance dwindled when the prince took charge of the empire.
- **Your Sentence:** ....

....

6. **DAUNT:**

- **Meaning:** Intimidate, dishearten; frighten.
- **Sentence:** Nothing could daunt the warrior from capturing the fort.

- **Your Sentence:** ....
  ....

7. **CONTAMINATE:**

- **Meaning:** To make something impure; to pollute; to adulterate.
- **Sentence:** The unhygienic villagers contaminated the drinking water.
- **Your Sentence:** ....
  ....

[C] Match the following:

	Words		*Meaning*
1.	Foist	(a)	attack
2.	Whittle	(b)	to lessen (in importance, etc.)
3.	Assault	(c)	try to make one accept something cheap, fake or ordinary, by pretending it to be very valuable, original or special.
4.	Connote	(d)	to intimidate; to dishearten.
5.	Dwindle	(e)	to reduce something by slicing it off repeatedly.
6.	Daunt	(f)	to pollute
7.	Contaminate	(g)	to mean or denote.

Answers: 1-c; 2-e; 3-a; 4-g; 5-b; 6-d; 7-f.

[D] Write words you have learnt in this chapter in front of their meanings.

1. To force one to accept something cheap or fake, by pretending it to be genuine or valuable:..................
2. To reduce something by cutting it repeatedly:.........

3. To attack:..

4. To signify or denote:...

5. To lessen (in importance):...

6. To intimidate:...

7. To make impure by adding impurities:....................

Answers: 1-foist; 2-whittle; 3-assault; 4-connote; 5-dwindle; 6-daunt; 7-contaminate.

Lesson Two

[A] Speak aloud the following words five times each

	Words	*Pronunciations*
1.	Repent	rɪ′pent
2.	Repel	rɪ′pel
3.	Nonplus	non′plʌs
4.	Replenish	rɪ′plenɪʃ
5.	Stigmatize	′stɪgmə,taɪz
6.	Burgeon	′bɜ:dz(ə)n
7.	Debilitate	dɪ′bɪlɪ,teɪt
8.	Extort	ɪk′stɔ:t

[B] Usage practice:

1. **REPENT:**
   - **Meaning:** Feel sorry for one's mistake and wish one had not done it; to regret:
   - **Sentence:** You will repent if you don't study properly.
   - **Your Sentence:** ....
   ....
2. **REPEL:**
   - **Meaning:** To drive away.
   - **Sentence:** The sight of bloodshed repelled the girls from the site of accident.

- **Your Sentence:** ....

  ....

3. **NONPLUS:**

- **Meaning:** To render shocked and speechless; to stun.
- **Sentence:** Whole world was nonplussed by the news of Rajiv Gandhi's assassination.
- **Your Sentence:** ....

  ....

4. **REPLENISH:**

- **Meaning:** To renew; to fill up (something empty) again.
- **Sentences:** (1) The commander requested the Government to replenish the stock of arms and ammunitions.

  (2) A grant from the Government replenished the depleted resources of the hospital.
- **Your Sentence:** ....

  ....

5. **STIGMATIZE:**

- **Meaning:** To put a mark of disgrace or shame [stigma is a mark of disgrace. Stigmatize means to put 'stigma' on someone, i.e. to mark someone with disgrace.]
- **Sentence:** The jealous competitors tried to stigmatize the reputation of the new, rising film star.
- **Your Sentence:** ....

  ....

6. **BURGEON:**

- **Meaning:** To flourish; to proliferate luxuriously.
- **Sentence:** (1) The new, talented actress burgeoned in the film industry.

  (2) The butterflies are eagerly awaiting the flowers to burgeon in my garden.
- **Your Sentence:** ....

  ....

7. **DEBILITATE:**

- **Meaning:** To weaken; to 'eat up' the strength of ; to make infirm.
- **Sentence:** Diarrhoea and malnutrition debilitates millions of children in India every year.
- **Your Sentence:** ....

  ....

8. **EXTORT:**

- **Meaning:** To 'twist out' forcibly.
- **Sentence:** The government is extorting very heavy taxes from the public.
- **Your Sentence:** ....

  ....

[C] Match the following:

Words		***Meanings***
1. Repent	(a)	to ward off; to drive away.
2. Repel	(b)	to shock and render speechless.
3. Nonplus	(c)	to 'twist out' forcibly.
4. Replenish	(d)	to regret
5. Stigmatize	(e)	to proliferate lavishly.
6. Burgeon	(f)	to weaken

7. Debilitate (g) to renew, or fill up again
8. Extort (h) to put a mark of shame.

Answers: 1-d; 2-a- 3-b- 4-g; 5-h; 6-e; 7-f; 8-c.

[D] Write down the words you have learnt in this lesson in front of their meanings.

1. To regret: ....
2. To drive away: ....
3. To shock and render speechless: ....
4. To fill up again: ....
5. To put a mark of disgrace on: ....
6. To flourish: ....
7. To 'eat up' the strength of: ....
8. To twist out forcibly: ....

Answers: 1-repent; 2-repel; 3-nonplus; 4-replenish; 5-stigmatize; 6-burgeon; 7-debilitate; 8-extort.

Lesson Three

[A] Pronounce the following words five times each

	Words	*Pronunciations*
1.	Waver	ʹweɪvə(r)
2.	Abound	əʹbaʊnd
3.	Exaggerate	ɪgʹzædzə,reɪt
4.	Incur	ɪnʹkɜ:(r)
5.	Muster	ʹmʌstə(r)
6.	Disgorge	dɪsʹgɔ:dz
7.	Disparage	dɪʹspærɪdz
8.	Pulverize	ʹpʌlvə,raiz

[B] Usage practice:

1. **WAVER:**
   - **Meaning:** Hesitate; become unsteady (while taking a decision).
   - **Sentence:** A good doctor never wavers in giving round-the-clock services to his patients.
   - **Your Sentence:** ....
     ....

2. **ABOUND:**
   - **Meaning:** To be in abundance/plenty.

- **Sentence:** U. P. and Haryana abound in sugarcane factories.
- **Your Sentence:** ....

....

3. **EXAGGERATE:**

- **Meaning:** To present a greater image of something which is much smaller or ordinary in reality.
- **Sentence:** Mothers usually exaggerate the achievements of their children.
- **Your Sentence:** ....

....

4. **INCUR:**

- **Meaning:** To reap the rewards/ results of one's own acts.
- **Sentence:** Joe incurred huge debts because of his extravagant nature.
- **Your Sentence:** ....

....

5. **MUSTER:**

- **Meaning:** To gather or collect.
- **Sentence:** (1) The dying warrior mustered all his strength to inflict the decisive blow on the enemy.
  (2) Jamshedpur Tata mustered all his resources to establish the Iron and Steel Industry.
- **Your Sentence:** ....

....

6. **DISGORGE:**

- **Meaning:** To emit out; to vomit.
- **Sentence:** The inspector forced the prisoner to disgorge the truth.

- **Your Sentence:** ....

....

7. DISPARAGE:

- **Meaning:** To speak with contempt (as if the other person is insignificant or worthless).
- **Sentence:** Raja Ram Mohan Roy disparaged the orthodox society in which women were treated as slaves.
- **Your Sentence:** ....

....

8. PULVERIZE:

- **Meaning:** To reduce to powder or thin pieces; to crush or destroy completely.
- **Sentence:** (1) The devil swore to pulverize humanity.

(2) Arjuna took a pledge to pulverize Duryodhana's army.

- **Your Sentence:** ....

....

[C] Match the following:

Words		***Meanings***
1. Waver	(a)	to be in plenty.
2. Abound	(b)	to get the result of one's own work.
3. exaggerate	(c)	to emit.
4. Incur	(d)	to speak with contempt (in order to bring down the reputation of someone).
5. Muster	(e)	to present an unreal, enlarged image of something.

6.	Disgorge	(f)	to hesitate.
7.	Disparage	(g)	to crush; to reduce to powder or thin pieces.
8.	Pulverize	(h)	to collect or gather.

Answers: 1-f; 2-a; 3-e; 4-b; 5-h; 6-c; 7-d; 8-g.

[D] Try to recall the words you have learnt in this chapter.

1.	....	:	to hesitate.
2.	....	:	to be in plenty.
3.	....	:	to present an enlarged image of something, while in reality the thing is much smaller or ordinary.
4.	....	:	to get the result of one's own deeds.
5.	....	:	to gather.
6	....	:	to emit.
7.	....	:	to speak with contempt (in order to bring down the reputation of someone)
8.	....	:	to crush, reduce to powder.

Answers: 1-waver; 2-abound; 3-exaggerate; 4-incur; 5-muster; 6-disgorge; 7-disparage; 8. pulverize.

Lesson Four

[A] Speak aloud the following words five time each

	Words	*Pronunciations*
1.	Confound	kən′faʊnd
2.	Cease	si:s
3.	Concede	kən′si:d
4.	Recall	rɪ′kɔ:l
5.	Implement	′ɪmplɪmənt
6.	Allay	ə′leɪ
7.	Adore	ə′dɔ: (r)

[B] Usage practice:

1. CONFOUND:

- **Meaning:** To throw into confusion.
- **Sentence:** The sudden arrival of the principal in the classroom confounded all the students.
- **Your Sentence:** ....

....

2. CEASE:

- **Meaning:** To stop.
- **Sentence:** Crime must cease and peace should prevail.

- **Your Sentence:** ....

  ....

3. **CONCEDE:**

- **Meaning:** To acknowledge (one's defeat etc.); to admit to be true.
- **Sentences:** 1. The enemy had to concede his defeat.

  2. Shyam had to concede that his work was inadequate.
- **Your Sentence:** ....

  ....

4. **RECALL:**

- **Meaning:** To bring back to memory.
- **Sentence:** I recalled my college days when I was young and beautiful.
- **Your Sentence:** ....

  ....

5. **IMPLEMENT:**

- **Meaning:** To bring into action.
- **Sentence:** Government is strictly implementing the new tax system to generate more funds.
- **Your Sentence:** ....

  ....

6. **ALLAY:**

- **Meaning:** To lessen the severity of; to relieve.
- **Sentence:** Meditation allays anxiety and fear.
- **Your Sentence:** ....

  ....

7. **ADORE:**

- **Meaning:** To love and admire greatly.

- **Sentence:** We must adore the courage of freedom fighters.
- **Your Sentence:** ....
....

[C] Match the following:

	Words		*Meanings*
1.	Confound	(a)	to stop
2.	Cease	(b)	to bring back to memory
3.	Concede	(c)	to throw into confusion.
4.	Recall	(d)	to love and admire immensely.
5.	Implement	(e)	to admit (one's failure etc.)
6.	Allay	(f)	to put into action.
7.	Adore	(g)	to relieve.

Answers: 1-c; 2-a; 3-e; 4-b; 5-f; 6-g; 7-d.

[D] Write the words you have learnt in this chapter in front of their meanings.

1. To throw into confusion : ....
2. To stop : ....
3. To admit (one's failure) ....
4. To bring back to memory :..
5. To put into action : ....
6. To relieve :...
7. To love and admire immensely :....................................

Answers: 1-confound; 2-cease; 3-concede; 4-recall; 5-implement; 6-allay; 7-adore.

Lesson Five

[A] Speak aloud the following words five times each

Words	*Pronunciations*
1. Lure	ɪʊə(r)
2. Convene	kən'vi:n
3. Exhilarate	ig'zɪlə,reɪt
4. Launch	ɪɔ:ntʃ
5. Agitate	'ædzɪ,teɪt
6. Mutilate	'mju:tɪ,leɪt
7. Cherish	'tʃerɪʃ

[B] Usage practice:

1 LURE:

- **Meaning:** To attract by throwing a bait (like money, reward, attractive career).
- **Sentence:** The glamour of Hollywood lured her into becoming an actress.
- **Your Sentence:** ....

  ....

2 CONVENE:

- **Meaning:** To call for (a meeting); to gather or assemble.
- **Sentence:** The director has convened a meeting on Saturday.

- **Your Sentence:** ....

....

3. **EXHILARATE:**
   - **Meaning:** To make happy.
   - **Sentence:** The success of the kidney transplant exhilarated the doctors.
   - **Your Sentence:** ....

   ....

4. **LAUNCH:**
   - **Meaning:** To send forth e.g. (a product in market; a new scheme; rocket, or missile into air etc.)
   - **Sentence:** The government has launched a new scheme to provide employment to the poor.
   - **Your Sentence:** ....

   ....

5. **AGITATE:**
   - **Meaning:** To stir up; to excite.
   - **Sentences:** (1) The assassination of Indira Gandhi agitated the public.

     (2) The leader agitated the crowd to burn the train.
   - **Your Sentence:** ....

   ....

6. **MUTILATE:**
   - **Meaning:** To damage or crush (parts of a body).
   - **Sentences:** (1) The police found a mutilated body in the field.

     (2) "Rats have mutilated all my books, mom!", the child yelled.
   - **Your Sentence:** ....

   ....

7. **CHERISH:**

- **Meaning:** To preserve (something beloved).
- **Sentence:** Many people still cherish their belief in ghosts.
- **Your Sentence:** ....

....

[C] Match the following:

	Words		*Meanings*
1.	Lure	(a)	to attract (by a bait).
2.	Convene	(b)	to preserve something beloved.
3.	Exhilarate	(c)	to send forth.
4.	Launch	(d)	to damage parts of a body.
5.	Agitate	(e)	to gather; to call for (a meeting).
6.	Mutilate	(f)	to stir up.
7.	Cherish.	(g)	to make happy.

Answers: 1-a; 2-e; 3-g; 4-c; 5-f; 6-d; 7-b.

[d] Write the words you have learnt in this chapter in front of their meanings.

1. To attract by a bait :..
2. To assemble, to call for (a meeting) :..............................
3. To make happy : ....
4. To send forth : ....
5. To stir up : ....
6. To damage parts of a body :..
7. To preserve something beloved :.......................................

Answers: 1-lure; 2-convene; 3-exhilarate; 4-launch; 5-agitate; 6-mutilate; 7-cherish.

Lesson Six

[A] Speak aloud the following words five times each.

Words		*Pronunciations*
1.	Extirpate	'ekstə,peɪt
2.	Covet	'kʌvɪt
3.	Wield	wi:ld
4.	Plunge	plʌndz
5.	Reinforce	,ri:n'ʃɔ:s
6.	Defy	diʃaɪ
7.	Demolish	dɪ'molɪʃ

[B] Usage practice:

1. **EXTIRPATE:**
   - **Meaning:** To destroy completely.
   - **Sentence:** Only good education can extirpate crime from the world.
   - **Your Sentence:** ....
     ....

2. **COVET:**
   - **Meaning:** To crave for something which belongs to someone else.
   - **Sentence:** Tapish covet's Maria's wealth.
   - **Your Sentence:** ....
     ....

3. **WIELD:**

- **Meaning:** (1) To hold something and use is.

  (2) To 'hold' a person and 'use' him according to one's wishes.

  (3) To exercise control over (others).

- **Sentence:** My mother is very skilful at wielding her authority over my father.
- **Your Sentence:** ....

  ....

4. **PLUNGE:**

- **Meaning:** To jump forcefully.
- **Sentence:** The diver plunged into the river to save the drowning child.
- **Your Sentence:** ....

  ....

5. **REINFORCE:**

- **Meaning:** To add strength to; to support.
- **Sentence:** The government reinforced the hospitals by providing them new hi-tech machines.
- **Your Sentence:** ....

  ....

6. **DEFY:**

- **Meaning:** Challenge and disobey.
- **Sentence:** The new student defied the unreasonable restrictions in the hostel.
- **Your Sentence:** ....

  ....

7. **DEMOLISH:**

- **Meaning:** To destroy by breaking or tearing apart.

- **Sentence:** The building was demolished according to the orders of the court.
- **Your Sentence:** ....

  ....

[C] Match the following:

	Words		*Meanings*
1.	Extirpate	(a)	to exercise control over
2.	Covet	(b)	to strengthen
3.	Wield	(c)	to jump forcefully
4.	Plunge	(d)	to destroy utterly
5.	Reinforce	(e)	to challenge and disobey
6.	Defy	(f)	to crave for something which belongs to someone else.
7.	Demolish	(g)	to break (a building etc.).

Answers: 1-d; 2-f; 3-a; 4-c; 5-b; 6-e; 7-g.

[D] Try to recall the words you have learnt in this chapter.

1. E.........: to destroy completely.
2. C.........: to crave to possess another's belongings.
3. W.........: to exercise control over.
4. P.........: to jump.
5. R.........: to strengthen.
6. D.........: to challenge and disobey.
7. D.........: to destroy by breaking (a building, monument, etc.).

Answers: 1-extirpate; 2-covet; 3-wield; 4-plunge; 5-reinforce; 6-defy; 7-demolish.

Lesson Seven

TEST YOUR PROGRESS

Please revise exercise 'B' of all the lessons discussed in this assignment before taking this test.

[A] Match the following:

	Words		*Meanings*
1.	Assault	(a)	to fill up again; to renew.
2.	Whittle	(b)	to call for (a meeting); to assemble.
3.	Replenish	(c)	to reduce by cutting repeatedly.
4.	Waver	(d)	do stop.
5.	Reinforce	(e)	to strengthen.
6.	Cease	(f)	to attack.
7.	Convene	(g)	to become unsteady; hesitate.
8.	Exhilarate	(h)	to jump forcefully.
9.	Covet	(i)	to make happy.
10.	Plunge	(j)	to long for other's possessions.

Answers: 1-f; 2-c; 3-a; 4-g; 5-e; 6-d; 7-b; 8-i; 9-j; 10-h.

[B] Match the following:

Words		*Meanings*	
1.	Nonplus	(a)	to destroy completely.
2.	Stigmatize	(b)	to render shocked and speechless.
3.	Incur	(c)	to attract by a bait.
4.	Recall	(d)	to bring back to memory.
5.	Confound	(e)	to collect or gather.
6.	Concede	(f)	to put a mark of shame.
7.	Lure	(g)	to exercise control over.
8.	Extirpate	(h)	to throw into confusion
9.	Wield	(i)	to get the result of one's own deeds.
10.	Muster	(j)	to admit (one's defeat or failure).

Answers: 1-b; 2-f; 3-i; 4-d; 5-h; 6-j; 7-c; 8-a; 9-g; 10-e.

Calculate your total marks by giving +1 for each correct answer, and adding them up.

Marks obtained.	*Remarks*
18-20	Excellent!
15-17	Very good
12-14	Good
8-11	Fair
5-7	Average
Below 5	Poor

Write the remark you got in this test in the circle provided below, with RED SKETCH PEN, in BOLD CAPITAL LETTERS.

This is the remark our student got in this test which shows how he/she is progressing through this course.

Words lead you to positions of prestige and power!

Assignment Six. . . Adjectives

Lesson One

[A] Speak aloud the following words five times each

Words	*Pronunciations*
1. Unanimous	ju:ˈnænɪməs
2. Ubiquitous	ju:ˈbɪkwɪtəs
3. Notorious	nəʊˈtɔ:rɪəs
4. Uncanny	ʌnˈkænɪ
5. Crotchety	ˈkrotʃɪtɪ
6. Diffident	ˈdɪfɪd(ə)nt
7. Effete	ɪˈfi:t

[B] Usage practice

1. **UNANIMOUS:**
   - **Meaning:** Agreed by all.
   - **Sentence:** The decision of giving free education to girls was unanimous.
   - Your Sentence:

2. **UBIQUITOUS:**
   - **Meaning:** Present everywhere.
   - **Sentence:** Grief is ubiquitous.
   - **Your Sentence:** ....
   ....

3. **NOTORIOUS:**

- **Meaning:** Mischievous.
- **Sentence:** (1) It is very difficult to treat the notorious pneumococcal infection.

  (2) Ashutosh was one of the most notorious students in my class.

4. **UNCANNY:**

- **Meaning:** Mysterious, eerie.
- **Sentence:** The uncanny atmosphere in the so-called haunted house made my sister uneasy.
- **Your Sentence:** ....

  ....

5. **CROTCHETY:**

- **Meaning:** Ill tempered.
- **Sentence:** "It is very difficult to please that crotchety old woman," my mom muttered.
- **Your Sentence:** ....

  ....

6. **DIFFIDENT:**

- **Meaning:** Lacking self confidence.
- **Sentence:** The examiner took pity on the diffident youths.
- **Your Sentence:** ....

  ....

7. **EFFETE:**

- **Meaning:** Weak. Exhausted, feeble
- **Sentence:** (1) Effete candidates were rejected in the competition.

  (2) The effete old man finally succumbed to his illness.

- **Your Sentence:** ....
  ....

[C] Match the following:

	Words		***Meanings***
1.	Unanimous	(a)	present everywhere.
2.	Ubiquitous	(b)	bad tempered.
3.	Notorious	(c)	mysterious.
4.	Uncanny	(d)	lacking self confidence.
5.	Crotchety	(e)	weak.
6.	Diffident	(f)	agreed by all.
7.	Effete.	(g)	mischievous.

Answers: 1-f; 2-a; 3-g; 4-c; 5-b; 6-d; 7-e.

[D] Write down the words you have learnt in this chapter in front of their meanings.

1. Agreed by all : ....
2. Present everywhere : ....
3. Mischievous : ....
4. Mysterious : ....
5. Bad tempered : ....
6. Lacking self confidence :..
7. Weak; vigourless :..

Answers: 1-unanimous; 2-ubiquitous; 3-notorious; 4-uncanny; 5-crotchety; 6-diffident; 7-effete.

Lesson Two

[A] Speak aloud the following words five times each

	Words	*Pronunciations*
1.	Wistful	\`wɪstʃʊl
2.	Serendipitious	ˌserənˈdɪpɪtəs
3.	Inclement	ɪnˈklemənt
4.	Vacant	\`veɪkənt
5.	Conciliatory	kən\`sɪlɪətərɪ
6.	Enamoured	ɪ\`næmərd
7.	Nefarious	nɪ\`feərɪəs

[B] Usage practice

1 **WISTFUL:**

- **Meaning:** Having intense yearning for.
- **Sentence:** The memories of the past made me wistful.
- **Your Sentence:** ....
  ....

2 **SERENDIPITOUS:**

- **Meaning:** Accidental and fortunate (discovery). This word is derived from 'serendipity' which means 'a gift of making discoveries luckily' by accident.

- **Sentence:** The serendipitous discovery of the treasure in the farm made the farmer insane.
- **Your Sentence:** ....

....

3. **INCLEMENT:**

- **Meaning:** Bad (weather)
- **Sentence:** The inclement weather prevented us from going out.
- **Your Sentence:** ....

....

4. **VACANT:**

- **Meaning:** (1) Empty.
- **Sentence:** The boys occupied the vacant seats in the picture hall.
- **Your Sentence:** ....

....

- **Meaning:** (2) Lacking sense, understanding, or interest (in surroundings, conversation, etc.)
- **Sentence:** When I enquired about his result, he gave me a vacant stare.
- **Your Sentence:** ....

....

5. **CONCILIATORY:**

- **Meaning:** Something (like, a remark) which overcomes or defeats the enmity or opposition.
- **Sentence:** The conciliatory remark by the principal, who was accused of being corrupt, made all his enemies silent.
- **Your Sentence:** ....

....

6. **ENAMOURED:**
   - **Meaning:** Inspired by love.
   - **Sentence:** The enamoured youth surmounted all the obstacles to marry his fiancé.
   - **Your Sentence:** ....

     ....

7. **NEFARIOUS:**
   - **Meaning:** Wicked; immoral.
   - **Sentence:** "Beware of the nefarious guys in the university" a father warned his son.
   - **Your Sentence:** ....

     ....

[C] Match the following:

	Words		*Meanings*
1.	Wistful	(a)	something which overcomes or defeats opposition.
2.	Serendipitous	(b)	having a sad yearning for
3.	Inclement	(c)	wicked
4.	Vacant	(d)	bad (weather)
5.	Conciliatory	(e)	inspired by love
6.	Enamoured	(f)	empty
7.	Nefarious	(g)	accidental and fortunate (discovery)

Answers: 1-b; 2-g; 3-d; 4-f; 5-a; 6-e; 7-c.

[D] Write the words you have learnt in this chapter in front of their meanings.

1. Having an intense yearning for : ....

2. Fortunate and accidental (discovery) :..........................
3. Bad (weather) : ....
4. Empty : ....
5. Something which defeats opposition :........................
6. Inspired by love : ....
7. Wicked; immoral : ....

Answers: 1-wistful; 2-serendipitous; 3-inclement; 4-vacant; 5-conciliatory; 6-enamoured; 7-nefarious.

Lesson Three

[A] Speak aloud the following words five times each

Words	*Pronunciations*
1. Unsavoury	ʌn`seIvərI
2. Reminiscent	,remInIs(ə)nt
3. Reliable	rIlaIəb(ə)l
4. Inebriated	I'ni:brI,eItId
5. Prominent	'promInənt
6. Pervasive	pə'veIsIv
7. Incorrigible	In'korIdzIb(ə)l

[B] Usage practice:

1. UNSAVOURY:

- **Meaning:** Distasteful.
- **Sentence:** (1) The husband threw away the unsavoury dish.

  (2) The unsavoury idea of making a house in the remote village was discarded.
- **Your Sentence:** ....

  ....

2. REMINISCENT:

- **Meaning:** The verb 'reminisce' means—to talk of or write about (and thus remind) some memories or past experiences. Reminiscent, the adjective, means—something which reminds.

- **Sentence:** The reminiscent remains of the bungalow made the landlord sentimental.
- **Your Sentence:** ....
....

3. **RELIABLE:**

- **Meaning:** Dependable; trustworthy.
- **Sentence:** I want a reliable business partner.
- **Your Sentence:** ....
....

4. **INEBRIATED:**

- **Meaning:** Drunk; deeply in the effect of alcohol.
- **Sentence:** (1) The inebriated driver landed up in an accident.

  (2) The girl viewed the inebriated boys with hatred.
- **Your Sentence:** ....
....

5. **PROMINENT:**

- **Meaning:** Conspicuous; highly noticeable.
- **Sentence:** (1) The prominent features of the business project were typed in bold, capital letters.

  (2) Everyone stared with awe at the prominent personalities in the cricket match.
- **Your Sentence:** ....
....

6. **PERVASIVE:**

- **Meaning:** Penetrating.

- **Sentence:** The pervasive desire to rise to the top made him work very hard.
- **Your Sentence:** ....
....

7. **INCORRIGIBLE:**

- **Meaning:** Which cannot be corrected or changed for the better.
- **Sentence:** Amputating a healthy limb is an incorrigible blunder.
- **Your Sentence:** ....
....

[C] Match the following:

	Words		*Meanings*
1.	Unsavoury	(a)	which cannot be corrected
2.	Reminiscent	(b)	a reminder
3.	Reliable	(c)	highly noticeable
4.	Inebriated	(d)	distasteful
5.	Prominent	(e)	penetrating
6.	Pervasive	(f)	dependable
7.	Incorrigible	(g)	drunk

Answers: 1-d; 2-b; 3-f; 4-g; 5-c; 6-e; 7-a.

[D] Try to recall the words you have learnt in this chapter:-

1. ....: distasteful.
2. ....: something that reminds.
3. ....: dependable.
4. ....: drunk.
5. ....: highly noticeable.

6. ....: penetrating.
7. ....: which is beyond correction or reform.

Answers: 1-unsavoury; 2-reminiscent; 3-reliable; 4-inebriated; 5-prominent; 6-pervasive; 7-incorrigible.

Lesson Four

[A] Speak aloud the following words five times each

Words	*Pronunciation*
1. Indignant	ɪn`dɪgnənt
2. Fortuitous	fɔ:`tju:ɪtəs
3. Sophisticated	sə`fɪstɪ,keɪtɪd
4. Sanguinary	`sæŋgwɪnərɪ
5. Stupendous	stju:`pendəs
6. Meticulous	mə`tɪkjʊləs
7. Abstruse	əb`stru:s

[B] Usage practice:

1. INDIGNANT:

- **Meaning:** Angry because of being unjustly injured (by an unfair comment, act etc.).
- **Sentence:** The indignant youth protested against the accusation that they are highly irresponsible and notorious.
- **Your Sentence:** ....

  ....

2. FORTUITOUS:

- **Meaning:** Occurring by good luck.
- **Sentence:** The fortuitous presence of doctors at the site of accident saved the victim's life.

- **Your Sentence:** ....

....

3. **SOPHISTICATED:**

- **Meaning:** Refined; cultured and complex; hi-tech.
- **Sentence:** (1) Society is becoming more and more sophisticated as the time is passing by.

  (2) Sophisticated medical instruments would improve the health services provided by the hospitals.
- **Your Sentence:** ....

....

4. **SANGUINARY:**

- **Meaning:** Accompanied by a lot of bloodshed.
- **Sentence:** Sanguinary battles do more harm than good to mankind.
- **Your Sentence:** ....

....

5. **STUPENDOUS:**

- **Meaning:** Very huge.
- **Sentence:** The stupendous Statue of Liberty inspires awe and admiration.
- **Your Sentence:** ....

....

6. **METICULOUS:**

- **Meaning:** Too much careful or fussy about details.
- **Sentence:** The meticulous sister-incharge kept records of everything happening in the dialysis department.
- **Your Sentence:** ....

....

7. **ABSTRUSE:**

- **Meaning:** Too complex and difficult to understand.
- **Sentence:** Doctors are famous for their abstruse hand writing.
- **Your Sentence:** ....

[C] Match the following:

	Words		*Meanings*
1.	Indignant	(a)	accompanied by blood-shed.
2.	Fortuitous	(b)	to much fussy about details.
3.	Sophisticated	(c)	angry because of being unjustly injured or insulted.
4.	Sanguinary	(d)	too complex and difficult to understand.
5.	Stupendous	(e)	refined.
6.	Meticulous	(f)	occurring by good luck
7.	Abstruse	(g)	huge

Answers: 1-c; 2-f; 3-e; 4-a; 5-g; 6-b; 7-d.

[D] Try to recall the words you have learnt in this chapter.

1. ....: angry because of being unjustly injured.
2. ....: happening by good luck.
3. Refined :.........
4. Accompanied by a lot of blood-shed :.........
5. Astonishingly huge :.........
6. Too much careful about details :.........
7. Too complex or difficult to understand :.........

Answers: 1-indignant; 2-fortuitous; 3-sophisticated; 4-sanguinary; 5-stupendous; 6-meticulous; 7-abstruse.

Lesson Five

[A] Speak aloud the following words five times each

Words	***Pronunciations***
1. Affluent	\`æflʊənt
2. Replete	rɪ\`pli:t
3. Compatible	kəm\`pætəb(ə)l
4. Vintage	\`vɪntɪdz
5. Contingent	kən\`tɪndz(ə)nt
6. Inscrutable	ɪn\`skru:təb(ə)l
7. Insouciant	ɪn\`su:sɪənt

[B] Usage practice:

1. AFFLUENT:

- **Meaning:** Rich.
- **Sentence:** Luxuries are meant for the affluent class.
- **Your Sentence:** ....

....

2 REPLETE:

- **Meaning:** Completely full; stuffed; engorged.
- **Sentence:** The replete stadium showed how interested the people were, in the match.
- **Your Sentence:** ....

....

3. **COMPATIBLE:**

- **Meaning:** Tolerant towards each other.
- **Sentence:** (1) A compatible life partner makes life easier and happier.

  (2) Only compatible blood can be transfused to a patient.
- **Your Sentence:** ....

  ....

4. **VINTAGE:**

- **Meaning:** The best.
- **Sentence:** (1) The vintage performance of Madhuri on stage in 1990 was highly applauded.

  (2) "My vintage period has gone! All that is left behind is frustration and despair", the old man winced.
- **Your Sentence:** ....

  ....

5. **CONTINGENT:**

- **Meaning:** Dependent on circumstance, situation, or events, likely to occur in future.
- **Sentence:** I don't rely on contingent schemes.
- **Your Sentence:** ....

  ....

6. **INSCRUTABLE:**

- **Meaning:** Impossible to penetrate, search or examine; too mysterious to solve.
- **Sentence:** Nancy Drew was baffled by the inscrutable mystery of the 99 steps.

- **Your Sentence:** ....

  ....

7. **INSOUCIANT:**

- **Meaning:** Carefree; unconcerned;
- **Sentence:** "You stupid, insouciant pig ! Your exams are on your head and you are still sleeping!" a mother scolded her son.
- **Your Sentence:** ....

  ....

[C] True/False.

	Words	*Meanings*	*True/False*
1.	Affluent	rich	....
2.	Replete	empty	....
3.	Compatible	intolerant	....
4.	Vintage	best	....
5.	Contingent	dependent on future circumstances	....
6.	Inscrutable	difficult to penetrate or solve	....
7.	Insouciant	concerned	....

Answers: 1-True; 2-False; 3-False; 4-True; 5-True; 6-True; 7-False.

[D] Try to recall the words you have learnt in this chapter.

1. .... : rich
2. .... : full
3. .... : tolerant
4. .... : best

5. .... : dependent on future circumstances

6. .... : which cannot be solved, too difficult to penetrate and search

7. .... : unconcerned

Answers: 1-affluent; 2-replete; 3-compatible; 4-vintage; 5-contingent; 6-inscrutable; 7-insouciant.

Lesson Six

[A] Speak aloud the following words five times each

	Words	***Pronunciations***
1.	Meagre	\`mi:gə(r)
2.	Posh	ρoʃ
3.	Jeopardous	\`dzepəd(ə)s
4.	Shabby	\`ʃæbɪ
5.	Acerbic	ə\`sɜ:bɪk
6.	Insalubrious	ˌɪnsə\`lu:briəs
7.	Infallible	ɪnfælɪb (ə)l

[B] Usage practice:

1 MEAGRE:

- **Meaning:** Very little; insufficient.
- **Sentence:** Private hospitals in India offer very meagre pay to nurses.
- **Your Sentence:** ....

....

2 POSH:

- **Meaning:** The rich; upper-class people.
- **Sentence:** Only the posh can afford to stay in five star hotels.
- **Your Sentence:** ....

....

3. JEOPARDOUS:

- **Meaning:** Dangerous; risky.
- **Sentence:** Sunny took part in the jeopardous car race last year.
- **Your Sentence:** ....

....

4. SHABBY:

- **Meaning:** Worn out or ruined in appearance.
- **Sentence:** The shabby beggars have stigmatized the reputation of our country.
- **Your Sentence:** ....

....

5. ACERBIC

- **Meaning:** Bitter and harsh (speech); pungent like an acid.
- **Sentence:** (1) Acerbic taste of vinegar repels me.

  (2) I was stunned by the acerbic tongue of the sweeper.
- **Your Sentence:** ....

....

6. INSALUBRIOUS:

- **Meaning:** Bad for health.
- **Sentence:** (1) I vacated the house because of its insalubrious location.

  (2) Many poor people live in the insalubrious slum areas.
- **Your Sentence:** ....

....

7. INFALLIBLE:

- **Meaning:** That which never goes wrong; that which never fails.
- **Sentence:** The commander formulated an infallible strategy to capture the enemy.
- **Your Sentence:** ....
....

[C] Match the following:

	Words		*Meanings*
1.	Meagre	(a)	dangerous
2.	Posh.	(b)	acidic or bitter
3.	Jeopardous	(c)	worn out or ruined in appearance
4.	Shabby	(d)	not good for health
5.	Acerbic	(e)	very little
6.	Insalubrious	(f)	unfailing
7.	Infallible	(g)	the rich, upper class people

Answers: 1-e; 2-g; 3-a; 4-c; 5-b; 6-d; 7-f.

[D] Try to recall the words you have learnt in this chapter.

1. ....: very little
2. ....: rich, upper, class
3. ....: dangerous
4. ....: worn out or ruined in appearance
5. ....: harsh; bitter
6. ....: bad for health.
7. ....: never-failing.

Answers: 1-meagre; 2-posh; 3-jeopardous; 4-shabby; 5-acerbic; 6-insalubrious; 7-infallible.

Lesson Seven

TEST YOUR PROGRESS

Revise exercise 'B' of all the lessons discussed in this assignment to score higher in this test.

[A] Match the following:

Words	*Meanings*
1. Unanimous	(a) mysterious; eerie
2. Uncanny	(b) dependable
3. Crotchety	(c) (an answer, remark etc.) which overcomes or defeats opposition
4. Serendipitous	(d) bloody
5. Conciliatory	(e) accidental, fortunate (discovery)
6. Reliable	(f) worn out or ruined in appearance
7. Fortuitous	(g) ill tempered
8. Sanguinary	(h) agreed by all
9. Shabby	(i) dangerous
10. Jeopardous	(j) occurring by good luck

[B] Match the following:

Words	*Meanings*
1. Ubiquitous	(a) rich
2. Notorious	(b) drunk

3. Wistful	(c) mischievous
4. Vacant	(d) empty
5. Unsavoury	(e) present everywhere
6. Inebriated	(f) huge
7. Stupendous	(g) tolerant
8. Compatible	(i) distasteful
9. Vintage	(j) best
10. Affluent	(k) a sad yearning for (the past, something lost).

Answers:

[A] 1-h; 2-a; 3-g; 4-e; 5-c; 6-b; 7-j; 8-d; 9-f; 10-i.

[B] 1-e; 2-c; 3-k; 4-d; 5-i; 6-b; 7-f; 8-g; 9-j; 10-a.

Calculate your marks:-

Give yourself +1 for each correct answer, and add them upto to get your score.

Marks obtained	***Remarks***
18-20	Excellent
15-17	Very good
12-14	Good
8-11	Fair
5-7	Average
Below 5	Poor

Write the remark you got in this test in the circle provided below with RED SKETCH PEN in BOLD, CAPITAL LETTERS.

This is the remark our student got in this test which shows how he/she is progressing through this course.

PART THREE

Good vocabulary makes people Listen to You!

ASSIGNMENT SEVEN. . . NOUN

Lesson One

[A] Speak aloud the following words five times each

	Words	*Pronunciations*
1.	Vehemence	\`vi:əməns
2.	Nonchalance	\`nonʃələns
3.	Ire	\`aɪə (r)
4.	Diatribe	\`daɪə,traɪb
5.	Logic	\`lodzɪk
6.	Condemnation	,kondem\`neiʃ(ə)n
7.	Rationale	,ræʃə\`na:l
8.	Malice	\`mælɪs
9.	Xenophobia	,zenə\`ʃəʊbɪə

[B] Usage practice:

1. VEHEMENCE:

- **Meaning:** A strong outburst of uncontrollable emotions.
- **Sentence:** The vehemence of the pleading woman softened the king's heart.
- **Your Sentence:** ....
  ....

2. NONCHALANCE:

- **Meaning:** Indifference.

- **Sentence:** The nonchalance of authorities towards their demands forced the labourers to go on strike.
- **Your Sentence:** ....
....

3. IRE:

- **Meaning:** Anger.
- **Sentence:** I fear the ire of my parents.
- **Your Sentence:** ....
....

4. DIATRIBE:

- **Meaning:** A violent verbal attack
- **Sentence:** The leader of the opposition party bombarded very indecent diatribe on the ruling party.
- **Your Sentence:** ....
....

5. LOGIC:

- **Meaning:** Reasoning.
- **Sentence:** Mahatama Gandhi had good logic behind every action.
- **Your Sentence:** ....
....

6. CONDEMNATION:

- **Meaning:** Expression of utter dislike; to show one's disapproval.
- **Sentence:** My father's condemnation of my smoking habit was strongly supported by my mother.
- **Your Sentence:** ....
....

7. RATIONALE:

- **Meaning:** A fundamental reason.
- **Sentence:** What is the rationale behind bunking classes?
- **Your Sentence:** ....

  ....

8. MALICE:

- **Meaning:** Ill-will.
- **Sentence:** Cassius' heart was full of malice for Julius Caesar.
- **Your Sentence:** ....

  ....

9. XENOPHOBIA

- **Meaning:** 'Xeno' means stranger, or foreigner; and 'phobia' means 'fear'.

  Xenophobia is fear (mixed with hatred) of strangers/foreigners.
- **Sentence:** Many people still have the deep seated xenophobia in their hearts.
- **Your Sentence:** ....

  ....

[C] Match the following:

Words		*Meanings*
1. Vehemence	(a)	expression of utter dislike
2. Nonchalance	(b)	reasoning
3. Ire	(c)	indifference
4. Diatribe	(d)	anger
5. Logic	(e)	a fundamental reason
6. Condemnation	(f)	a violent verbal attack

7.	Rationale	(g)	fear of strangers
8.	Malice	(h)	strong outburst of uncontrollable emotions.
9.	Xenophobia	(i)	ill-will

Answers: 1-h; 2-c; 3-d; 4-f; 5-b; 6-a; 7-e; 8-i; 9-g.

[D] Try to recall the words you have learnt in this chapter.

1. Strong outburst of uncontrollable emotions :...........
2. Indifference :..
3. Anger: ....
4. A violent verbal attack :...
5. Reasoning : ....
6. Expression of utter disapproval or dislike :...........
7. A fundamental reason: ....
8. Ill-will : ....
9. Fear of strangers : ....

Answer: a-vehemence; 2-nonchalance; 3-Ire; 4-diatribe; 5-logic; 6-condemnation; 7-rationale; 8-malice; 9-xenophobia.

Lesson Two

[A] Speak aloud the following words five times each

	Words	*Pronunciations*
1.	Arsenal	\`a:sən (ə)l
2.	Solace	\`soləs
3.	Menace	\`menɪs
4.	Prerogative	prɪ\`rogətɪv
5.	Catastrophe	kə\`tæstrəfɪ
6.	Execution	,eksɪ\`kju:ʃ (ə)n
7.	Macabre	mə\`ka:br
8.	Zenith	\`zenɪθ

[B] Usage practice:

1 ARSENAL:

- **Meaning:** (1) Collection of weapons.
- **Sentence:** Every country maintains a huge arsenal to combat enemies.
- **Your Sentence:** ....

  ....
- **Meaning:** (2) Resources of something comparable to a huge collection of deadly weapons (like abuses mischiefs etc.)
- **Sentence:** (2) Vineeta attacked the loafers with a huge arsenal of abuses.

- **Your Sentence:** ....

  ....

2. SOLACE:

- **Meaning:** Peace; comfort (in times of distress)
- **Sentence:** Sister Mathew seeks solace in the church whenever she is in distress.
- **Your Sentence:** ....

  ....

3. MENACE:

- **Meaning:** A continuous source of trouble.
- **Sentence:** Denis is a menace.
- **Your Sentence:** ....

  ....

4. PREROGATIVE:

- **Meaning:** (Advantage, power etc.) given only to some special persons.
- **Sentence:** Children enjoy the prerogative of being the first to be saved in times of emergency.
- **Your Sentence:** ....

  ....

5. CATASTROPHE:

- **Meaning:** Misfortune; disaster.
- **Sentence:** The gulf war was a catastrophe man would never forget.

  Adjective 'catastrophic' means 'that which causes widespread disaster.
- **Sentence:** Japan is a land of catastrophic earthquakes.
- **Your Sentence:** Catastrophe (noun):

Catastrophic (adjective):

6. EXECUTION:

- **Meaning:** Carrying out or implementing (ones plans, etc.)
- **Sentence:** The execution of five year plans brought about tremendous development in India.
- **Your Sentence:** ....
....

7. MACABRE:

- **Meaning:** Horrible (like a decayed dead body).
- **Sentence:** I was shocked to see the macabre road traffic accident.
- **Your Sentence:** ....
....

8. ZENITH:

- **Meaning:** The highest point.
- **Sentence:** Hritik Roshan promises to achieve the zenith of success in the film industry.
- **Your Sentence:** ....
....

[C] Match the following:

	Words		*Meanings*
1.	Arsenal	(a)	special powers or advantages given to special people.
2.	Solace	(b)	horrible
3.	Menace	(c)	a huge collection of (weapons)
4.	Prerogative	(d)	a sudden widespread disaster
5.	Catastrophe	(e)	comfort; peace

6. Execution	(f) continuous source of trouble
7. Macabre	(g) the highest point
8. Zenith	(h) carrying out (one's plans, etc.)

Answers: 1-c; 2-e; 3-f; 4-a; 5-d; 6-h; 7-b; 8-g.

[D] Write the words you have learnt in this chapter in front of their meanings.

1. A huge collection of weapons : ....
2. Peace : ....
3. A continuous source of trouble : ....
4. Special powers given to special people : ....
5. Widespread disaster/misfortune : ....
6. Carrying out (one's plans, etc.) : ....
7. Horrible : ....
8. The highest point : ....

Answers: 1-arsenal; 2-solace; 3-menace; 4-prerogative; 5-catastrophe; 6-execution; 7-macabre; 8-zenith.

Lesson Three

[A] Speak aloud the following words five times each

Words	*Pronunciations*
1. Avenue	\`ævə,nju:
2. Acme	\`ækmɪ
3. Conspiracy	kən\`spɪrəsɪ
4. Insanity	ɪn\`sænɪtɪ
5. Replica	\`replɪkə
6. Uproar	\`ʌprɔ: (r)
7. Commotion	kə\`məʊʃ(ə)n
8. Paucity	\`pɔ:sɪtɪ

[B] Usage practice:

1 AVENUE:

- **Meaning:** (1) A broad road with regularly spaced trees on either side.

  (2) A way (of solving a problem; of earning money; etc.).
- **Sentence** (1) There is tight security on the avenue leading to the president's house.

  (2) Joe knows many avenues of earning money.
- **Your Sentence:(1)**..

  ....

(2) ....

....

2 ACME:

- **Meaning:** The highest point
- **Sentence:** Rajiv Gandhi wanted India to reach the acme of scientific developments.
- **Your Sentence:** ....

....

3. CONSPIRACY:

- **Meaning:** A carefully devised secret plan for committing a crime (like murder, sabotage, etc.).
- **Sentence:** Brutus joined hands with Cassius in the conspiracy against Julius Caesar.
- **Your Sentence:** ....

....

4. INSANITY:

- **Meaning:** (1) Madness; mental derangement.

  (2) Extreme foolishness (equivalent to madness)
- **Sentence:** (1) It was my insanity which led me to the path of self destruction.

  (2) "Did you say Venktesh is selling all his property for a few coins! My God! It must be his insanity, nothing else!," the old man exclaimed.
- **Your Sentence:** ....

....

5. REPLICA:

- **Meaning:** An exact copy.
- **Sentence:** Has any sculptor ever dared to make a replica of Statue of Liberty?

- **Your Sentence:** ....
  ....

6. UPROAR:

- **Meaning:** Noisy disturbance; (like a violent roar).
- **Sentence:** An uproar reverberated in the stadium when Sachin Tendulkar completed his century.
- **Your Sentence:** ....
  ....

7. COMMOTION

- **Meaning:** (1) Noisy disturbance.
- **Sentence:** The assassination of Julius Caesar resulted in an uncontrollable commotion on the streets of Rome.
- **Your Sentence:** ....
  ....
- **Meaning:** (2) Agitation.
- **Sentence:** The implementation of new taxes created a commotion in the public.
- **Your Sentence:** ....
  ....

8. PAUCITY

- **Meaning:** Scarcity.
- **Sentence:** (1) I could not answer all the questions in the exam due to paucity of time.

  (2) Millions of people came forward to replenish the paucity of food and medicines in the flooded area.
- **Your Sentence:** ....
  ....

[C] Match the following:

Words		*Meanings*
1. Avenue	(a)	noisy disturbance; agitation
2. Conspiracy	(b)	a way (of earning money, solving a problem etc.).
3. Replica	(c)	an exact copy
4. Commotion	(d)	a carefully devised secret plan to commit a crime

Answers: 1-b; 2-d; 3-c; 4-a.

[D] Match the following:

Words		*Meanings*
1. Acme	(a)	noisy (like a roar). disturbance
2. Insanity	(b)	scarcity
3. Uproar	(c)	the highest point
4. Paucity	(d)	madness; extreme foolishness

Answer: 1-c; 2-d; 3-a; 4-b.

[E] Try to recall the words you have learnt in this chapter.

1. AV
2. AC
3. CON
4. IN
5. RE
6. UP
7. COM
8. PA

Answers: 1-avenue; 2-acme; 3-conspiracy; 4-insanity; 5-replica; 6-uproar; 7-commotion; 8-paucity.

Lesson Four

[A] Speak aloud the following words five times each

	Words	*Pronunciations*
1.	Venture	\`ventʃə(r)
2.	Umbrage	ʌmbrIdz
3.	Repository	rI\`pozitərI
4.	Flair	\`fleə(r)
5.	Turmoil	\`t3:mɔIl
6.	Propaganda	,propə\`gændə
7.	Abduction	əb\`dʌkʃ(ə)n
8.	Climax	\`klaImæks
9.	Altercation	ɔ:ltə\`keIʃ(ə)n
10.	Quandary	\`kwondərI

[B] Usage practice:

1. VENTURE:

- **Meaning:** A dangerous or risky undertaking.
- **Sentence:** The businessman is spending 10 crore rupees in the new venture.
- **Your Sentence:** ....

....

2. UMBRAGE:

- **Meaning:** Displeasure or resentment because of being injured (physically or emotionally). Take umbrage: feel offended. The word has been derived from the french word 'umbra' which means shadow; so, when a person takes umbrage it means he has taken a 'shadow' on himself (because of being hurt or injured by something bad—like an insult, scolding, injustice, etc.

- **Sentence:** The cricket team took umbrage at the biased decisions of the umpire.
- **Your Sentence:** ....

....

3. REPOSITORY:

- **Meaning:** Repository is a place where things are deposited or stored e.g. a museum is a repository of antiques: books are repositories of information; even a person may be a repository of some secrets or information.
- **Sentence:** Books are the best repositories of useful information.
- **Your Sentence:** ....

....

4. FLAIR:

- **Meaning:** Talent or ability.
- **Sentence:** The editors have a flair of judging the value of different scripts.
- **Your Sentence:** ....

....

5. TURMOIL:

- **Meaning:** Agitation.
- **Sentence:** Turmoil followed the terrible bomb explosion in the city.

- **Your Sentence:** ....

  ....

6. PROPAGANDA:

- **Meaning:** An organized spread of news on information.
- **Sentence:** There was a lot of propaganda about the love affair.
- **Your Sentence:** ....

  ....

7. ABDUCTION:

- **Meaning:** The act of kidnapping; taking away of something.
- **Sentence:** The abduction of the girl was strongly condemned.
- **Your Sentence:** ....

  ....

8. CLIMAX:

- **Meaning:** The point of highest intensity (of emotions, interest etc.).
- **Sentence:** The climax of the story held the readers spell bound.
- **Your Sentence:** ....

  ....

9. ALTERCATION:

- **Meaning:** Hot argument.
- **Sentence:** The two business partners had a terrible altercation regarding the share in profits.
- **Your Sentence:** ....

  ....

10. QUANDARY:

- **Meaning:** A difficult, disagreeable situation.
- **Sentence:** The criminals found themselves in a quandary when the police surrounded them from all sides.
- **Your Sentence:** ....
  ....

[C] Match the following.

	Words		*Meanings*
1.	Venture	(a)	agitation
2.	Umbrage	(b)	an organized spread of news or information
3.	Repository	(c)	a risky undertaking
4.	Flair	(d)	a point of highest intensity (of emotions, interest, etc.).
5.	Turmoil	(e)	resentment or displeasure
6.	Propaganda	(f)	talent
7.	Abduction	(g)	a difficult and hateful situation
8.	Climax	(h)	the act of kidnapping
9.	Altercation	(i)	a place where things are stored or deposited
10.	Quandary	(j)	a violent argument

Answers: 1-c; 2-e; 3-i; 4-f; 5-a; 6-b; 7-h; 8-d; 9-j; 10-g.

[D] Try to recall the words you have learnt in this chapter.

1. A risky undertaking : ....
2. A 'shadow' of displeasure on being offended or hurt :

3. A place where things are stored : ....
4. Talent : ....
5. Agitation : ....
6. An organized spread of information : ....
7. Kidnapping : ....
8. Point of highest intensity (of emotions, interest, etc.) :

   ....

9. A violent argument : ....
10. A difficult and hateful situation : ....

Answers: 1-venture; 2-umbrage; 3-repository; 4-flair; 5-turmoil; 6-propaganda; 7-abduction; 8-climax; 9-altercatron; 10-quandary.

Lesson Five

[A] Speak aloud the following words five times each

	Words	*Pronunciations*
1.	Savour	\`seɪvə (r)
2.	Inkling	\`ɪŋklɪŋ
3.	Expiry	ɪk\`spaɪərɪ
4.	Protest	\`prəʊtest
5.	Tussle	\`tʌs(ə)l
6.	Portfolio	pɔ:t\`fəʊlɪəʊ
7.	Zeal	zi:l
8.	Nemesis	\`nemɪsɪs
9.	Anathema	ə\`næθəmə
10.	Charlatan	\`ʃa:lət(ə)n

[B] Usage practice:

1 SAVOUR:

- **Meaning:** A characteristic taste, smell or flavour.
- **Sentence:** The savour of honey is irresistible.
- **Your Sentence:** ....

....

2 INKLING:

- **Meaning:** A slight idea; hint or suspicion.

- **Sentence:** The police officer got an inkling of his senior's involvement in the crime, so he decided to study the whole case again.
- **Your Sentence:** ....
....

3. EXPIRY:

- **Meaning:** Death.
- **Sentence:** Always check the expiry date of a medicine before taking it.

  The boy was very much upset by the news of expiry of his father.
- **Your Sentence:(Verb)** ....
....

  (Noun) ....
....

4. PROTEST:

- **Meaning:** Firm declaration of objection (noun)

  To object strongly (verb)
- **Sentence:** (Noun): The protest of the students against the new reservation bill was strongly praised in the newspapers.

  (Verb): The tenant protested against the deceitful tricks of the shrewd landlord.
- **Your Sentence:** ....
....

5. TUSSLE:

- **Meaning:** A rough struggle.
- **Sentence:** The longstanding ego based tussle between the husband and wife led to divorce.

- **Your Sentence:** ....
....

6. **PORTFOLIO:**

- **Meaning:** (1) A flat case which contains samples of an artist's work.
- **Sentence:** (1) After seéing the artist's portfolio, the director accepted his paintings for exhibition.
- **Your Sentence:** ....
....
- **Meaning:** (2) A minister's field of responsibility.
- **Sentence:** (2) The ministers were given portfolios according to their choices.
- **Your Sentence:** ....
....
- **Meaning:** (3) The list of investment.
- **Sentence:** I was amazed to see the huge portfolio of investments of my father.

7. **ZEAL:**

- **Meaning:** Great eagerness or interest; enthusiasm.
- **Sentence:** The air hostess had amazing zeal in entertaining the passengers.
- **Your Sentence:** ....
....

8. **NEMESIS:**

- **Meaning:** Nemesis' is the Greek goddess of vengeance. She punishes the wrong to restore justice in this world. In common use, 'nemesis' means vengeance or punishment given by a victim or victim's supporters to a criminal. [The plural of nemesis is nemeses.]

- **Sentence:** The freedom fighters had only one goal —nemesis.
- **Your Sentence:** ....
  ....

9. **ANATHEMA:**

- **Meaning:** An object of intense dislike or hatred.
- **Sentence:** Bigamy or polygamy is considered an anathema in Indian society.
- **Your Sentence:** ....
  ....

10. **CHARLATAN:**

- **Meaning:** A quack
- **Sentence:** Health minister is very much worried about the deceitful charlatans fooling the innocent villagers.
- **Your Sentence:** ....
  ....

[C] Match the following:-

	Words		***Meanings***
1.	Savour	(a)	a flat case containing. samples of art of an artist.
2.	Inkling	(b)	a quack.
3.	Expiry	(c)	a firm declaration of objection.
4.	Protest	(d)	great interest.
5.	Tussle	(e)	a rough struggle.
6.	Portfolio	(f)	death.
7.	Zeal	(g)	a hateful thing.
8.	Nemesis	(h)	a hint on suspicion.
9.	Anathema	(i)	a characteristic flavour.

10. Charlatan (j) revenge taken by a victim or his supporters.

Answers: a-i; 2-h; 3-f; 4-c; 5-e; 6-a; 7-d; 8-j; 9-g; 10-b.

[D] Try to recall the words you have learnt in this chapter.

1. A characteristic flavour : ....
2. A guess or suspicion : ....
3. Death or end : ....
4. A firm declaration of objection : ....
5. A rough struggle : ....
6. An area of responsibility of a minister : ....
7. Great eagerness or interest : ....
8. Vengeance : ....
9. A very hateful thing : ....
10. A quack : ....

Answers: 1-savour; 2-inkling; 3-expiry; 4-protest; 5-tussle; 6-portfolio; 7-zeal; 8-nemesis; 9-anthema; 10-charlatan.

Lesson Six

[A] Speak aloud the following words five times each

	Words	*Pronunciations*
1.	Core	kɔ:(r)
2.	Parity	'pærɪtɪ
3.	Compulsions	kəm'pʌlʃ(ə)n
4.	Initiative	ɪ'nɪʃətɪv
5.	Query	'kwɪərɪ
6.	Moratorium	,morə'tɔ:rɪəm
7.	Complacency	kəm'pleɪsənsɪ
8.	Blandishments	'blændɪʃmənt
9.	Oblivion	ə'blɪvɪən

[B] Usage practice:

1. CORE

- **Meaning:** (1) The central portion.
- **Sentence:** (1) The core of the earth is very hot.
- **Your Sentence:** ....

   ....

- **Meaning:** (2) Central or essential part.
- **Sentence:** (2) The terrible car accident shook the very core of my heart.

(3) The great financial loss shook the very core of his industry.

- **Your Sentence:** ....

....

2. PARITY:

- **Meaning:** Equal level or status.
- **Sentence:** Aruna claimed parity with Shobha in the field of studies, but could not prove it.
- **Your Sentence:** ....

....

3. COMPULSION:

- **Meaning:** An irresistible pressure.
- **Sentence:** A sensible person acts by reason, not under compulsions.
- **Your Sentence:** ....

....

4. INITIATIVE:

- **Meaning:** (1) The ability to initiate or begin.
- **Sentence:** (1) Dr. Sunanda lacks the initiative to begin kidney transplantations in the hospital.
- **Your Sentence:** ....

....

- **Meaning:** (2) The first step/move.
- **Sentence:** The girls in the classroom took the initiative to educate the villagers.
- **Your Sentence:** ....

....

5. QUERY

- **Meaning:** A question; doubt.
- **Sentence:** Children have a lot of queries regarding everything.

- **Your Sentence:** ....

   ....

6. MORATORIUM:

- **Meaning:** A legal ban.
- **Sentence:** Government is observing a moratorium on the sale of mustard oil because of the spread of dropsy.
- **Your Sentence:** ....

   ....

7. COMPLACENCY:

- **Meaning:** Peace and self satisfaction.
- **Sentence:** (1) Complacency is not a slave of wealth.
   (2) Many people lack complacency in this materialistic world.
- **Your Sentence:** ....

   ....

8. BLANDISHMENTS:

- **Meaning:** cajolery; persuasion by flattery.
- **Sentence:** Many industrialists depend on blandishments to gain political favours.
- **Your Sentence:** ....

   ....

9. OBLIVION:

- **Meaning:** State of being forgotten.
- **Sentence:** Many huge empires fell into oblivion as years passed by.
- **Your Sentence:** ....

   ....

   Oblivious (adjective) followed by 'to' or of means 'unaware (of).

- **Sentence:** It was a shame that the king was completely oblivious of the sufferings of the poor.

- **Your Sentence:** ....

....

[C] Match the following:

	Words		*Meanings*
1.	Core	(a)	equal level
2.	Parity	(b)	persuasion by flattery
3.	Compulsion	(c)	the central or most important part.
4.	Initiative	(d)	a question or doubt
5.	Query	(e)	a state of being completely forgotten
6.	Moratorium	(f)	ability to initiate or begin.
7.	Complacency	(g)	a legal ban
8.	Blandishment	(h)	self satisfaction or peace of mind.
9.	Oblivion	(i)	an irresistible pressure

Answers: 1-c; 2-a; 3-i; 4-f; 5-d; 6-g; 7-h; 8-b; 9-e.

[D] Write down the words you have learnt in this chapter in front of their meanings.

1. The central part : ....
2. Equal status : ....
3. An irresistible pressure : ....
4. Ability to initiate : ....
5. A question : ....
6. A legal ban : ....
7. Self satisfaction : ....
8. Persuasion by flattery : ....
9. A state of being forgotten : ....

Answers: 1-core; 2-parity; 3-compulsion; 4-initiative; 5-query; 6-moratorium; 7-complacency; 8-blandishment; 9-oblivion.

Lesson Seven

TEST YOUR PROGRESS

Revise the chapters exercise 'B' discussed in this assignment before taking this test so that you may score well.

You may take this test now-

[A] Match the following:

	Words		*Meanings*
1.	Avenue	(a)	a flat case having samples of art of an artist
2.	Insanity	(b)	a broad road lined by trees on either side
3.	Umbrage	(c)	central or most important part
4.	Venture	(d)	feeling of resentment or displeasure
5.	Turmoil	(e)	a risky undertaking
6.	Savour	(f)	self satisfaction or peace of mind.
7.	Portfolio	(g)	madness
8.	Core	(h)	a characteristic flavour
9.	Moratorium	(i)	ban
10.	Complacency	(j)	violent agitation

[B] Fill in the blanks using following words at appropriate places.

Complacency, query, zeal, abduction, commotion.

1. An uncontrollable .... followed the bomb explosion. [the word means a confused and noisy disturbance].
2. The .... of the minister's daughter was strongly condemned [the word means taking away of].
3. The student raised a stupid .... [the word means: a question or doubt].
4. .... in medicine has made him a good doctor [the word means great interest or eagerness].
5. .... is the essence of happiness [the word means 'self satisfaction'].

[C] True/False.

	Words	*Meanings*	*True/False*
1.	Ire	pleasure	....
2.	Rationale	reasoning fundamental	....
3.	Nonchalance	indifference	....
4.	Solace	peace	....
5.	Catastrophe	the trophy of a cat-walk fashion show.	....

Answers:

[A] 1-b; 2-g; 3-d; 4-e; 5-j; 6-h; 7-a; 8-c; 9-i; 10-f.

[B] 1-commotion; 2-abduction; 3-query; 4-zeal 5-complacency.

[C] 1-false; 2-true; 3-true; 4-true; 5-false.

Calculate your marks

Give yourself +1 for each correct answer and calculate your total marks by adding them up.

Marks obtained	***remarks***
17-20	Excellent
14-16	Very good
12-13	Good
8-11	Fair
5-7	Average
Below 5	Poor

Write the remark you got in this test in the circle provided below with RED SKETCH PEN in BOLD CAPITAL LETTERS.

This is the remark our student got in this test which indicates how he/she is progressing through this course.

Personality glows with good vocabulary!

ASSIGNMENT EIGHT. . . VERBS

Lesson One

[A] Speak aloud the following words five times each

Words	*Pronunciations*
1. Flare	fleə(r)
2. Disrupt	dis`r^pt
3. Accentuate	æk`sentjʊ,eit
4. Inveigle	in`veig(ə)l
5. Endorse	in`dɔ:s
6. Elope	i`leʊp
7. Accomplish	ə`k^mlIʃ

[B] Usage practice:

1 **FLARE:**

- **Meaning:** (1) To burn with a bright, unsteady flame.
- **Sentence:** (1) The cigarette tip flared up on touching the flame.
- **Your Sentence:** ....

  ....

- **Meaning** (2) To 'burn' in wild anger.
- **Sentence:** (2) The principal flared up on seeing the fashionable youths.
- **Your Sentence:** ....

  ....

2 DISRUPT:

- **Meaning:** To break apart.
- **Sentence:** Misunderstandings can easily disrupt good relationships.
- **Your Sentence:** ....

....

3. ACCENTUATE:

- **Meaning:** To emphasise; to give stress to.
- **Sentence:** The doctors accentuate the importance of hygiene and balanced diet.
- **Your Sentence:** ....

....

4. INVEIGLE:

- **Meaning:** To persuade cunningly (to attract, trap, or get a work done from a person).
- **Sentence:** Rahul tried to inveigle Reema into marriage, but could not succeed.
- **Your Sentence:** ....

....

5. ENDORSE:

- **Meaning:** To agree; to give one's consent or approval.
- **Sentence:** The view of the scientist endorsed the theory of relativity.
- **Your Sentence:** ....

....

6. Elope:

- **Meaning:** To run away secretly (to marry).

- **Sentence:** The lovers eloped last night to get married.
- **Your Sentence:** ....

....

7. ACCOMPLISH:

- **Meaning:** To complete (a task).
- **Sentence:** We must accomplish this task on time.
- **Your Sentence:** ....

....

[C] Match the following:

	Words		***Meanings***
1.	Flare	(a)	to break apart
2.	Disrupt	(b)	to agree
3.	Accentuate	(c)	to burn
4.	Inveigle	(d)	to run away secretly
5.	Endorse	(e)	to finish (a task)
6.	Elope	(f)	to emphasise
7.	Accomplish	(g)	to persuade cunningly

Answers: 1-c; 2-a; 3-f; 4-g; 5-b; 6-d; 7-e.

[D] Try to recall the words you have learnt in this chapter.

1. F
2. D
3. A ....E
4. I
5. EN
6. EL
7. A........H

Answers: 1-Flare; 2-Disrupt; 3-Accentuate; 4-Inveigle; 5-Endorse; 6-Elope; 7-Accomplish.

Lesson Two

[A] Speak aloud the following words five times each

Words	*Pronunciations*
1. Grope	grəʊp
2. Retrieve	rɪ`tri:v
3. Coerce	kəʊ`ɜ:s
4. Clamour	`klæmə (r)
5. Hamper	`hæmpə (r)
6. Eradicate	ɪ`rædɪ,keɪt
7. Accrue	ə`kru:

[B] Usage practice:

1 GROPE:

- **Meaning:** To search by feeling (as searching in the dark).
- **Sentence:** Babloo groped for his torch in the dark on hearing the strange sound in his room.
- **Your Sentence:** ....

....

2. RETRIEVE:

- **Meaning:** To bring back into better or healthier state.
- **Sentence:** These days the Government is trying to

retrieve the dilapidated historical monuments. [dilapidated: ruined].

- **Your Sentence:** ....

....

3. **COERCE:**

- **Meaning:** To force.
- **Sentence:** "Please don't coerce me to marry that fat girl, mom!," the boy pleaded.
- **Your Sentence:** ....

....

4. **CLAMOUR:**

- **Meaning:** (1) To make a loud, persistent noise.
- **Sentence:** (1) The machines clamoured in the industry from morning to evening.
- **Your Sentence:** ....

....

- **Meaning** (2) To protest, or make demands, loudly and persistently.
- **Sentence:** (2) The labourers clamoured before the industrialist to increase their wages.
- **Your Sentence:** ....

....

5. **HAMPER:**

- **Meaning:** To obstruct.
- **Sentence:** (1) Your laziness would hamper your own progress

  (2) The strike hampered the plans of the industrialist
- **Your Sentence:** ....

....

6. ERADICATE

- **Meaning:** To eliminate completely; to destroy completely.
- **Sentence**: WHO has launched a world-wide campaign to eradicate poliomyelitis
- **Your Sentence:** ....

  ....

7. ACCRUE:

- **Meaning:** To gather.
- **Sentence:** By toilsome labour the farmer accrued one lakh rupees to marry his daughter.
- **Your Sentence:** ....

  ....

[C] Match the following:

	Words		*Meanings*
1.	Grope	(a)	to make a loud, persistent noise
2.	Retrieve	(b)	to search by feeling (in the dark)
3.	Coerce	(c)	to gather
4.	Clamour	(d)	to obstruct
5.	Hamper	(e)	to eliminate completely
6.	Eradicate	(f)	to revive, or bring back into healthy state.
7.	Accrue	(g)	to force

Answers: 1-b; 2-f; 3-g; 4-a; 5-d; 6-e; 7-c.

[D] Write down the words you have learnt in this chapter in front of their meanings.

1. To search by feeling (as if in the dark):..........................
2. To bring back into healthy state again:..........................
3. To force: ....
4. To make loud, persistent noise:......................................
5. To obstruct: ....
6. To eliminate completely: ....
7. To collect or gather: ....

Answers: 1-grope; 2-retrieve; 3-coerce; 4-clamour; 5-hamper; 6-eradicate; 7-accrue.

Lesson Three

[A] Speak aloud the following words five times each

Words	*Pronunciations*
1. Rupture	\`rʌptʃə (r)
2. Accommodate	ə\`komə,deɪt
3. Devour	dɪ\`vaʊə (r)
4. Commemorate	kə\`memə,reɪt
5. Encounter	ɪn\`kaʊntə (r)
6. Expedite	\`ekspɪ,daɪt
7. Haunt	hɔ:nt

[B] Usage Practice

1. RUPTURE:

- **Meaning:** To break or tear.
- **Sentence:** (1) The balloon ruptured with a terrible sound.

  (2) The bomb explosion ruptured the flesh of the soldiers.
- **Your Sentence:** ....

  ....

2 ACCOMMODATE:

- **Meaning:** To adjust something (inside a room etc.).
- **Sentence:** The manager tried to accommodate all of us in the hotel.

- **Your Sentence:** ....

....

3. DEVOUR:

- **Meaning:** To destroy (as it by eating); to eat up greedily.
- **Sentence:** The hungry children devoured the whole cake within a few minutes!
- **Your Sentence:** ....

....

4. COMMEMORATE:

- **Meaning:** To honour (a person or event); to keep a memory alive.
- **Sentence:** On Dussehra we commemorate the occasion of Lord Rama's victory over the evil forces.
- **Your Sentence:** ....

....

5. ENCOUNTER:

- **Meaning:** To meet or face someone (in a battle, fight etc.).
- **Sentence:** The policemen encountered the criminals and arrested all of them.
- **Your Sentence:** ....

....

6. EXPEDITE:

- **Meaning:** To speed up.
- **Sentences:** (1) Medicines expedite recovery of a patient.

  (2) It is very difficult to expedite the proceeding of a court.

- **Your Sentence:** ....

....

7. HAUNT:

- **Meaning:** To trouble by persisting in thoughts or memory.
- **Sentence:** The thought of being punished for my mistake haunted me day and night.
- **Your Sentence:** ....

....

[C] Match the following:

	Words		*Meanings*
1.	Rupture	(a)	to honour in order to keep alive its memories.
2.	Accommodate	(b)	to meet face to face.
3.	Devour	(c)	to break or tear apart
4.	Commemorate	(d)	to speed up
5.	Encounter	(e)	to adjust (in a room, etc).
6.	Expedite	(f)	to trouble by persisting in thoughts or memory
7.	Haunt	(g)	to destroy by eating.

Answers: 1-c; 2-e; 3-g; 4-a; 5-b; 6-d; 7-f.

[D] Write down the words you have learnt in this chapter in front of their meanings.

1. To break or tear : ....
2. To adjust inside : ....
3. To destroy by eating : ....
4. To honour so as to keep one's memory alive : ....
5. To meet or face : ....

6. To hasten : ....

7. To trouble by persisting in thoughts :............................

Answers: 1-rupture; 2-accommodate; 3-devour; 4-commemorate; 5-encounter; 6-expedite; 7-haunt.

Lesson Four

[A] Speak aloud the following words five times each

	Words	*Pronunciations*
1.	Rehabilitate	,ri:hə'bɪlɪ,teɪt
2.	Convince	kən`vɪns
3.	Estrange	ɪ`streɪndz
4.	Persuade	pə`sweɪd
5.	Enervate	`enə,veɪt
6.	Incriminate	ɪn`krɪmɪ,neɪt
7.	Lacerate	`læsə,reɪt
8.	Accustom	ə`kʌstəm

[B] Usage practice:

1. REHABILITATE:

- **Meaning:** To restore to the original healthy condition, or to the best possible condition (physically, emotionally and socially).
- **Sentence:** We must try to rehabilitate handicapped people.
- **Your Sentence:** ....

  ....

2 CONVINCE:

- **Meaning:** To make someone believe something by putting forward arguments, proofs, etc.

- **Sentence:** I convinced my teacher that I was really out of station the previous day.
- **Your Sentence:** ....
....

3. **ESTRANGE:**

- **Meaning:** To withdraw, or turn away, one's love, affection from a person, who was once very dear.
- **Sentence:** My wife has estranged me because I betrayed her.
- **Your Sentence:** ....
....

4. **PERSUADE:**

- **Meaning:** To make one do something by arguments, flattery, etc.
- **Sentence:** The salesmen try to persuade customers to buy their products.
- **Your Sentence:** ....
....

5. **ENERVATE:**

- **Meaning:** To weaken.
- **Sentence:** The little girl got enervated by the sight of the terrible accident.
- **Your Sentence:** ....
....

6. **INCRIMINATE:**

- **Meaning:** To involve in crime.
- **Sentence:** The new evidence has incriminated many cricket players in the match fixing case.
- **Your Sentence:** ....
....

7. LACERATE:

- **Meaning:** (1) To tear apart.
- **Sentence:** (1) The fall lacerated the skin of the old man.
- **Your Sentence:** ....

  ....

- **Meaning:** (2) Hurt or wounded emotionally. i.e. feelings can also be 'torn apart'.
- **Sentence:** (2) The indifference of the girl lacerated the feelings of her lover.
- **Your Sentence:** ....

  ....

8. ACCUSTOM:

- **Meaning:** To make 'used to' or habitual.
- **Sentence:** Initially children find it very difficult to accustom themselves to the hostel life.
- **Your Sentence:** ....

  ....

[C] Match the following:

Words		*Meanings*
1. Rehabilitate	(a)	to involve in the accusation of crime.
2. Convince	(b)	to weaken
3. Estrange	(c)	to restore to normal or healthy way of life.
4. Enervate	(d)	To treat a known and dear person as if he/she were a stranger.
5. Incriminate	(e)	to tear apart.
6. Lacerate	(f)	to persuade

7. Accustom (g) to make someone 'used to' something.

Answers: 1-c; 2-f; 3-d; 4-b; 5-a; 6-e; 7-g.

[D] Write the words you have learnt in this chapter in front of their meanings.

1. To restore to normal, or near normal state:...................
2. To persuade (by giving proofs, arguments, etc.): ....
   ....
3. To treat a dear person as if he/she were a stranger:...
   ....
4. To weaken: ....
5. To involve someone in the accusation of crime:.........
6. To tear apart: ....
7. To make habitual or used to: ....

Answers: 1-rehabilitate; 2-convince; 3-estrange; 4-enervate; 5-incriminate; 6-lacerate; 7-accustom.

Lesson Five

[A] Speak aloud the following words five times each.

Words	*Pronunciations*
1. Emphasize	\`emfə,saɪz
2. Abandon	ə\`bænd(ə)n
3. Embark	ɪm\`ba:k
4. Foil	fɔɪl
5. Befit	bɪ\`fɪt
6. Nurture	\`nɜ:tʃə (r)
7. Yearn	jɜ:n
8. Obliterate	ə\`blɪtə,reɪt

[B] Usage practice

1. **EMPHASIZE:**
   - **Meaning:** To stress; to lay special importance on.
   - **Sentence:** The doctor emphasized the importance of family planning in front of the villagers.
   - **Your Sentence:** ....

   ....

2 **ABANDON:**
   - **Meaning:** To give up completely.
   - **Sentences:** (1) Somya has abandoned all hopes of restoring peace in her family.

(2) Arun abandoned all his bad habits once he married Kiran.

- **Your Sentence:** ....

....

3. EMBARK:

- **Meaning:** (1) To board a ship or boat.

  (2) 'Ride on' (a new scheme, project, etc), i.e. start working on (a scheme).

  (3) 'Ride' (a person to achieve one's goal) i.e. to take help of (an important person who can make one successful).

- **Sentences:** (1) I embarked on the bus to reach Dudhwa park.

  (2) The young boys embarked upon an ambitious project.

  (3) The young doctor embarked upon his seniors to establish in Lucknow.

- **Your Sentence:** ....

  (2)

  (3)

4. FOIL:

- **Meaning:** To destroy or ruin.
- **Sentence:** Indian soldiers foiled the secret plans of attack of the enemy.
- **Your Sentence:** ....

....

5. BEFIT:

- **Meaning:** To be suitable.
- **Sentence:** "Your house befits my peace loving nature, sir," the new tenant said.

- **Your Sentence:** ....

....

6. NURTURE:

- **Meaning:** To support or encourage the growth and development of.
- **Sentence:** Despite the hardships, the nurse nurtured her children very nicely.
- **Your Sentence:** ....

....

7. YEARN:

- **Meaning:** To long for; to have an intense desire to get something.
- **Sentence:** Sheeba yearns to marry a prince.
- **Your Sentence:** ....

....

8. OBLITERATE:

- **Meaning:** To wipe out or destroy.
- **Sentence:** The criminal obliterated all his finger prints before leaving the site of crime.
- **Your Sentence:** ....

....

[C] Match the following:

Words	*Meanings*
1. Emphasize	(a) to start working (on a project).
2. Abandon	(b) to support the growth and development of.
3. Embark	(c) to give stress to.
4. Foil	(d) to be suitable.

5.	Befit	(e)	to wipe out (e.g. finger prints etc.)
6.	Nurture	(f)	to give up.
7.	Yearn	(g)	to ruin (a plan etc.).
8.	Obliterate.	(h)	to long for.

Answers: 1-c; 2-f; 3-a; 4-g; 5-d; 6-b; 7-h; 8-e.

[D] Write the words you have learnt in this chapter in front of their meanings.

1. To lay special importance on:..
2. To give up completely: ....
3. To "ride upon": ....
4. To ruin, (a plan): ....
5. To be suitable:...
6. To support the growth and development of:................
7. To long for:..
8. To wipe out (fingerprints, etc.):......................................

Answers: 1-emphasize; 2-abandon; 3-embark; 4-foil; 5-befit; 6-nurture; 7-yearn; 8-obliterate.

Lesson Six

[A] Speak aloud the following words five times each.

Words	*Pronunciations*
1. Dispel	di`spel
2. Clarify	`klæri,faI
3. Resume	ri`zju:m
4. Undermine	,^ndə`maIn
5. Exacerbate	ek`sæsè,beIt
6. Offend	ə`fend
7. Pacify	'pæsI,faI
8. Penetrate	'penI,treIt

[B] Usage practice:

1. **DISPEL:**

- **Meaning:** To disperse or scatter.
- **Sentence:**

  The annoyed gardener dispelled the children away. The assurance from my mother, dispelled my fears about my failure in the exams.

- **Your Sentence:** ....

  ....

2. **CLARIFY:**

- **Meaning:** To make clear.

- **Sentence:** The couple clarified all the misunderstandings between them to restore peace in their home.
- **Your Sentence:** ....

....

3. RESUME:

- **Meaning:** To take back again (one's position, work, seat, etc.).
- **Sentence:** The president resumed his work as soon as he returned from Australia.
- **Your Sentence:** ....

....

4. UNDERMINE:

- **Meaning:** To weaken, or destroy the base of something gradually.
- **Sentence:** (1) The enemy is trying to undermine our country by spoiling our young generations.

  (2) The sea waves have undermined the rocks.
- **Your Sentence:** ....

....

5. EXACERBATE:

- **Meaning:** To make worse or more bitter.
- **Sentence:** Rupas rudeness has exacerbated her already bad relations with her husband.
- **Your Sentence:** ....

....

6. OFFEND:

- **Meaning:** To annoy
- **Sentence:** The unruly students offended the

teachers by passing indecent comments.

- **Your Sentence:** ....

....

7. PACIFY:

- **Meaning:** To calm down.
- **Sentence:** The parents tried to pacify the anger of their child.
- **Your Sentence:** ....

....

8. PENETRATE:

- **Meaning:** To enter inside.
- **Sentence:** The bullet penetrated the target with ease.
- **Your Sentence:** ....

....

[C] Match the following:

Words		*Meanings*
1. Dispel	(a)	to weaken the base of something gradually
2. Clarify	(b)	to calm down.
3. Resume	(c)	to make worse or more bitter.
4. Undermine	(d)	to take back again (one's work, position, etc.).
5. Exacerbate	(e)	to annoy.
6. Offend	(f)	to make clear
7. Pacify	(g)	to enter inside forcibly
8. Penetrate.	(h)	to scatter or disperse.

Answers: 1-h; 2-f; 3-d; 4-a; 5-c; 6-e; 7-b; 8-g.

[D] Try to recall the words you have learnt in this chapter. Hints have been given to help you.

1. To disperse: D ....
2. To make clear: C..
3. To take back again (one's position, etc.): R..................
4. To make more bitter: E ....
5. To annoy: O ....
6. To calm down: Pa ....
7. To enter inside forcibly: Pe ....

Answers: 1-dispel; 2-clarify; 3-resume; 4-exacerbate; 5-offend; 6-pacify; 7-penetrate.

Lesson Seven

TEST YOUR PROGRESS

Revise exercise 'B' of the chapters discussed in this assignment before taking this test to get more marks.

[A] Match the following:

Words		*Meanings*
1. Flare	(a)	to run away secretly.
2. Disrupt	(b)	to burst in wild anger.
3. Inveigle	(c)	to meet face to face.
4. Elope	(d)	to destroy by eating
5. Estrange	(e)	to restore to the best possible condition.
6. Retrieve	(f)	to being back to better or healthier state.
7. Devour	(g)	to break apart.
8. Encounter	(h)	to persuade (into a trap).
9. Rehabilitate	(i)	to treat someone beloved coldly, as if he/she were a stranger.

[B] Match the following:

Words		*Meanings*
1. Accentuate	(a)	to force

2.	Endorse	(b)	to agree to
3.	Grope	(c)	to search by feeling (as in the dark)
4.	Coerce	(d)	to give up completely
5.	Accomplish	(e)	to make more bitter
6.	Rupture	(f)	to ride on
7.	Abandon	(g)	to scatter
8.	Embark	(h)	to break or tear
9.	Dispel	(i)	to make more prominent
10.	Exacerbate	(j)	to complete.

Answers:

[A] 1-b; 2-g; 3-h; 4-a; 5-i; 6-f; 7-d; 8-c; 9-e.

[B] 1-i; 2-b; 3-c; 4-a; 5-j; 6-h; 7-d; 8-f; 9-g; 10-e.

Calculate your marks:

Give yourself +1 for each correct answer, and add them up to get your score.

Marks obtained	***Remarks***
16-20	Excellent
14-15	Very good
12-13	Good
8-11	Fair
5-7	Average
below 5	Poor.

Write the remark you got in this test in the circle provided below in BOLD, CAPITAL LETTERS with RED SKETCH PEN.

This is the remark our student got in this test which indicates how he/she is progressing through this course.

Good Vocabulary means winning half the battle beforehand!

ASSIGNMENT NINE. . . ADJECTIVES.

Lesson One

[A] Speak aloud the following words five times each

	Words	*Pronunciations*
1.	Acrimonious	,ækrɪ`məʊnɪəs
2.	Captious	`kæpʃəs
3.	Tremendous	trɪ`mendəs
4.	Discernible	dɪ`sɜ:nɪb(ə)l
5.	Furtive	`fɜ:tɪv
6.	Gracious	`greɪʃəs
7.	Parsimonious	,pa:sɪ`məunɪəs

[B] Usage practice.

1. ACRIMONIOUS:

- **Meaning:** Sour or bitter exceedingly rude (speech, behaviour, etc.)
- **Sentence:** "Watch your tongue, young lady! I would not tolerate your acrimonious speech," the shopkeeper threatened.
- **Your Sentence:** ....

....

2. CAPTIOUS:

- **Meaning:** Fault-finder i.e. a person who keeps finding faults with everything.

- **Sentence:** Never marry a captious lady if you want to live in peace.
- **Your Sentence:** ....

....

3. TREMENDOUS:

- **Meaning:** Huge.
- **Sentence:** You need tremendous will-power to become an ascetic.
- **Your Sentence:** ....

....

4. DISCERNIBLE:

- **Meaning:** Clear and legible; easy to understand.
- **Sentence:** Discernible handwriting fetches better marks in examinations.
- **Your Sentence:** ....

....

5. FURTIVE:

- **Meaning:** Secretive; stealthy.
- **Sentence:** The boy saw the girl he loved with a furtive glance before going out of the classroom.
- **Your Sentence:** ....

....

6. GRACIOUS:

- **Meaning:** Polite and courteous; kind and merciful (especially towards inferior people).
- **Sentence:** The gracious queen distributed alms to the poor.
- **Your Sentence:** ....

....

7. PARSIMONIOUS:

- **Meaning:** Stingy; thrifty.
- **Sentence:** The parsimonious businessman never offers even a cup of tea to anyone.
- **Your Sentence:** ....
....

[C] Match the following:

	Words		*Meanings*
1.	Acrimonious	(a)	legible
2.	Captious	(b)	stingy
3.	Tremendous	(c)	kind and courteous
4.	Discernible	(d)	secretive
5.	Furtive	(e)	huge
6.	Gracious	(f)	fault-finder
7.	Parsimonious	(g)	bitter (speech or manner)

Answers: 1-g; 2-f; 3-e; 4-a; 5-d; 6-c; 7-b.

[D] Try to recall the words you have learnt in this chapter.

1 Sour, bitter or exceedingly bad (speech or manner) : A ....

2. Fault-findes: C ....

3. Huge: T ....

4. Legible: D ....

5. Secretive: F ....

6. Merciful and polite: G ....

7. Stingy: P ....

Answers: 1-acrimonious; 2-captious; 3-tremendous; 4-discernible; 5-furtive; 6-gracious; 7-parsimonious.

Lesson Two

[A] Speak aloud the following words five times each

	Words	*Pronunciations*
1.	Potable	`pəʊtəb (ə)l
2.	Frantic	`fræntɪk
3.	Garish	`geərɪʃ
4.	Exuberant	ig`zju:bərənt
5.	Adamant	`ædəmənt
6.	Dilapidated	dɪlæpɪ,deɪtɪd
7.	Atrocious	ə`trəʊʃəs

[B] Usage practice:

1. POTABLE:

- **Meaning:** Drinkable.
- **Sentence:** Potable water must be provided in rural areas too.
- **Your Sentence:** ....

....

2 FRANTIC:

- **Meaning:** In wild excitement (simulating madness)
- **Sentence:** His frantic efforts to earn money gave him a bad reputation.

- **Your Sentence:** ....

  ....

3. **GARISH:**

- **Meaning:** Pretentious; showy; gaudy.
- **Sentence:** The neo-rich made a garish display of his money.
- **Your Sentence:** ....

  ....

4. **EXUBERANT :**

- **Meaning:** (1) Jovial; playful
- **Sentence:** (1) The victorious boys were exuberant and full of mischief when they returned back from the match.
- **Your Sentence:** ....

  ....

- **Meaning:** (2) Growing luxuriously.
- **Sentence:** (2) The exuberant vegetation of Dehradun attracts tourists.
- **Your Sentence:** ....

  ....

5. **ADAMANT:**

- **Meaning:** Stubbornly determined.
- **Sentence:** Mrs. Daisy was adamant on the point that she had seen a ghost.
- **Your Sentence:** ....

  ....

6. **DILAPIDATED**

- **Meaning:** In worn-out or ruined condition.
- **Sentence:** It was a pity to see the dilapidated house in the village.

- **Your Sentence:** ....
....

7. **ATROCIOUS:**
   - **Meaning:** Extremely wicked bad.
   - **Sentence:** The atrocious behaviour of the shopkeeper was disliked by the customers.
   - **Your Sentence:** ....
....

[C] Match the following:

	Words		*Meanings*
1.	Potable	(a)	In wild excitement
2.	Frantic	(b)	Showy
3.	Garish	(c)	Wicked
4.	Exuberant	(d)	Drinkable
5.	Adamant	(e)	In worn-out or ruined condition
6.	Dilapidated	(f)	Lively
7.	Atrocious	(g)	Stubbornly sticking, obstinately determined.

Answers: 1-d; 2-a; 3-b; 4-f; 5-g; 6-e; 7-c.

[D] Write the words you have learnt in this chapter in front of their meanings.

1. Drinkable: P..
2. In wild excitement: F..
3. Showy or gaudy: G..
4. Lively: E..
5. Stubbornly determined: A..

6. In worn-out condition: D ....
7. Extremely wicked: A ....

Answers: 1-potable; 2-frantic; 3-garish; 4-exuberant; 5-adamant; 6-dilapidated; 7-atrocious.

Lesson Three

[A] Speak aloud the following words five times each.

	Words	*Meanings*
1.	Affable	\`æfəb(ə)l
2.	Callous	\`kæləs
3.	Inevitable	ɪn\`evɪtəb(ə)l
4.	Stray	streɪ
5.	Transient	\`trænzɪənt
6.	Prosaic	prə\`zeɪɪk

[B] Usage practice:

1. AFFABLE:

- **Meaning:** Kind and friendly (especially to inferior people).
- **Sentence:** Patients look for an affable and caring doctor.
- **Your Sentence:** ....

....

2 CALLOUS:

- **Meaning:** Hardened and insensitive (e.g. to feelings).
- **Sentence:** (1) The vagabond's feet became callous by walking bare-footed on rough roads.

- **Your Sentence:** ....

  ....

- **Sentence** (2) "Her callous heart loves me not!" a lover wailed.

- **Your Sentence:** ....

  ....

3. INEVITABLE:

- **Meaning:** Unavoidable.

- **Sentence:** Disaster is inevitable if pollution remains unchecked.

- **Your Sentence:** ....

  ....

4. STRAY:

- **Meaning:** One who has deviated from the right path (or the path of good morals).

- **Sentence:** Stray gangsters are a source of continuous trouble for the public.

- **Your Sentence:** ....

  ....

5. TRANSIENT:

- **Meaning:** Occurring temporarily.

- **Sentence:** The transient emotional upset after the failure soon blew away.

- **Your Sentence:** ....

  ....

6. PROSAIC:

- **Meaning:** Dull, unattractive or unromantic [i.e. something that lacks poetic beauty, and is like a prose-dull and unromantic.

- **Sentence:** (1) Prosaic faces should not choose modelling as a career.

  (2) The prosaic old generation keeps on finding faults with everything.

- **Your Sentence:** ....

  ....

[C] Match the following:

	Words		*Meanings*
1.	Affable	(a)	unavoidable.
2.	Callous	(b)	deviated from the right path.
3.	Inevitable	(c)	kind and friendly.
4.	Stray	(d)	temporary.
5.	Transient	(e)	dull and unattractive.
6.	Prosaic	(f)	hardened and insensitive.

Answers: 1-c; 2-f; 3-a; 4-b; 5-d; 6-e.

[D] Write the words you have learnt in this chapter in front of their meanings.

1. Kind and friendly: A ....
2. Hardened and insensitive:

   C ....

3. Unavoidable: I..........................
4. Deviated from the right path: S..........................
5. Temporary: T ....
6. Dull, unattractive and unromantic: P ....

Answers: 1-affable; 2-callous; 3-inevitable; 4-stray; 5-transient; 6-prosaic.

Lesson Four

[A] Speak aloud the following words five times each

Words	*Pronunciations*
1. Exemplary	ig`zempləri
2. Enormous	inɔ:məs
3. Crucial	`kru:ʃ(ə)l
4. Invincible	in`vinsib(ə)l
5. Irrational	i`ræʃən(ə)l
6. Kaleidoscopic	kə,ləidə`skopik
7. Agile	`ædzail

[B] Usage practice:

1. EXEMPLARY:

- **Meaning:** Fit to be given as an example; a representative of (some work, etc.).
- **Sentence:** Mother Teresa has given exemplary services to the poor.
- **Your Sentence:** ....

....

2 ENORMOUS:

- **Meaning:** Huge.
- **Sentence:** The child got frightened on seeing the enormous size of the elephant.

- **Your Sentence:** ....

  ....

3. **CRUCIAL:**

- **Meaning:** Critical, indispensable; very important.
- **Sentence:** Every child needs advice of elders during the crucial time of choosing a career.
- **Your Sentence:** ....

  ....

4. **INVINCIBLE:**

- **Meaning:** Unconquerable; that which cannot be defeated.
- **Sentence:** (1) HIV remains invincible so far.

  (2) The fort of Chittor was considered to be invincible.
- **Your Sentence:** ....

  ....

5. **IRRATIONAL:**

- **Meaning:** Unreasonable; baseless.
- **Sentence:** Irrational decisions lead to failures and losses.
- **Your Sentence:** ....

  ....

6. **KALEIDOSCOPIC:**

- **Meaning:** Colourful and attractive.
- **Sentence:** The children enjoyed the kaleidoscopic view of the valley from the cliff.
- **Your Sentence:** ....

  ....

7. **AGILE:**

- **Meaning:** Quick and active.
- **Sentence:** The agile thief quickly disappeared into the forest.
- **Your Sentence:** ....
....

[C] Match the following:

	Words		*Meanings*
1.	Exemplary	(a)	critical
2.	Enormous	(b)	unconquerable
3.	Crucial	(c)	quick
4.	Invincible	(d)	huge
5.	Irrational	(e)	fit to be taken as an example
6.	Kaleidoscopic	(f)	unreasonable, baseless
7.	Agile	(g)	colourful.

Answers: 1-e; 2-d; 3-a; 4-b; 5-f; 6-g; 7-c.

[D] Write down the words you have learnt in this chapter in front of their meanings.

1. Fit to be taken as an example: Ex ....
2. Huge: En ....
3. Critical: C ....
4. Unconquerable: In ....
5. Unreasonable: Ir ....
6. Colourful and attractive: K ....
7. Quick: A ....

Answers: 1-exemplary; 2-enormous; 3-crucial; 4-invincible; 5-irrational; 6-kaleidoscopic; 7-agile.

Lesson Five

[A] Speak aloud the following words five times each

	Words	*Pronunciations*
1.	Jingoistic	,dzɪŋgəʊ`ɪstɪk
2.	Vitriolic	, vɪtrɪ`olɪk
3.	Spurious	`spjʊərɪəs
4.	Ridiculous	rɪ`dɪkjʊləs
5.	Hackneyed	`hæknɪd
6.	Ravenous	`rævənəs
7.	Abject	`æbdzekt

[B] Usage practice:

1 JINGOISTIC:

- **Meaning:** War-loving.
- **Sentence:** Equatorial forests are a home of many jingoistic tribes.
- **Your Sentence:** ....

....

2 VITRIOLIC:

- **Meaning:** Hostile; full of enmity or bitterness.
- **Sentence:** (1) Unhealthy family atmosphere engenders vitriolic feelings in children.

- **Your Sentence:** ....

  ....

- **Sentence:** (2) The years of imprisonment choked the vitriolic feelings of the criminal.
- **Your Sentence:** ....

  ....

3. SPURIOUS:

- **Meaning:** False; unauthentic.
- **Sentence:** The candidate submitted spurious information to gain access to the examination.
- **Your Sentence:** ....

  ....

4. RIDICULOUS:

- **Meaning:** Absurd and laughable.
- **Sentence:** "Don't you think your idea of chasing a tiger by a wooden stick is ridiculous?," the girl mocked of her boyfriend.
- **Your Sentence:** ....

  ....

5. HACKNEYED:

- **Meaning:** Become ordinary, worn-out, or stale because of too many repetitions.
- **Sentence:** The children became bored by the hackneyed old tricks in the circus.
- **Your Sentence:** ....

  ....

6. RAVENOUS:

- **Meaning:** Very hungry and extortionate, (like or raven).

- **Sentence:** The ravenous dogs devoured the dead body within minutes.
- **Your Sentence:** ....
....

7. **ABJECT:**

- **Meaning:** Utterly low or miserable.
- **Sentence:** Beggars live in abject poverty.
- **Your Sentence:** ....
....

[C] Match the following:

Words		*Meanings*
1. Jingoistic	(a)	absurd and laughable.
2. Vitriolic	(b)	war-loving
3. Spurious	(c)	utterly low and miserable
4. Ridiculous	(d)	false
5. Hackneyed	(e)	hostile
6. Ravenous	(f)	very hungry and extortionate
7. Abject	(g)	rendered stale, worn-out and uninteresting due to frequent repetitions.

Answers: 1-b; 2-e; 3-d; 4-a; 5-g; 6-f; 7-c.

[D] Write the words you have learnt in this chapter in front of their meanings.

1. One who loves war: ....
2. Hostile: ....
3. False: ....
4. Absurd and laughable: ....

5. Rendered worn out, unattractive, and stale due to too many repetitions: ....

6. Too hungry and extortionate: ....

7. Too low and miserable: ....

Answers: 1-jingoistic; 2-vitriolic; 3-spurious; 4-ridiculous; 5-hackneyed; 6-ravenous; 7-abject.

Lesson Six

[A] Speak aloud the following words five times each

	Words	*Pronunciations*
1.	Bizarre	bɪ`za:(r)
2.	Unscrupulous	ʌn`skru:pjʊləs
3.	Futile	`fju:taɪl
4.	Fabulous	`fæbjʊləs
5.	Incredible	ɪn`kredɪb(ə)l
6.	Drastic	`dræstɪk
7.	Serene	sɪ`ri:n

[B] Usage practice:

1. **BIZARRE:**

   - **Meaning:** Odd or strange in appearance.
   - **Sentence:** (1) The bizarre vagabond in the hotel attracted attention.

     (2) The Young generation has bizarre dreams in their eyes.
   - **Your Sentence:** ....

     ....

2. **UNSCRUPULOUS:**

   - **Meaning:** Unprincipled.
   - **Sentence:** I never trust unscrupulous people.

- **Your Sentence:** ....

 ....

3. FUTILE:

- **Meaning:** Useless
- **Sentence:** All his efforts to save his honour in the court proved futile.
- **Your Sentence:** ....

 ....

4. FABULOUS:

- **Meaning:** Marvellous (like a fable).
- **Sentence:** I saw a fabulous waterfall in Bangalore.
- **Your Sentence:** ....

 ....

5. INCREDIBLE:

- **Meaning:** Unbelievable
- **Sentence:** "It is incredible !," the girl exclaimed on seeing a space ship in the field.
- **Your Sentence:** ....

 ....

6. DRASTIC:

- **Meaning:** That which causes severe and widespread effects.
- **Sentence:** Ignorance and illiteracy have drastic effects on the development of a country.
- **Your Sentence:** ....

 ....

7. SERENE:

- **Meaning:** Calm.

- **Sentence:** There is a serene atmosphere near the coast.
- **Your Sentence:** ....
....

[C] Match the following:

	Words		*Meanings*
1.	Bizarre	(a)	unbelievable
2.	Unscrupulous	(b)	marvellous (like a fable)
3.	Futile	(c)	odd or strange in appearance
4.	Fabulous	(d)	that which causes widespread and severe effects
5.	Incredible	(e)	unprincipled
6.	Drastic	(f)	useless
7.	Serene	(g)	calm

Answers: 1-c; 2-e; 3-f; 4-b; 5-a; 6-d; 7-g.

[D] Write down the words you have learnt in this chapter in front of their meanings.

1. Old or strange looking:..
2. Unprincipled:..
3. Useless: ....
4. Marvellous: ....
5. That which causes severe and widespread effects:......
....
6. Calm and peaceful:..
7. Unbelievable: ....

Answers: 1-bizarre; 2-unscrupulous; 3-futile; 4-fabulous; 5-drastic; 6-serene; 7-incredible.

Lesson Seven

TEST YOUR PROGRESS

Revise exercise B in the chapters discussed in this assignment before taking this test, so that you may score well.

[A] Match the Following:

	Words		*Meanings*
1.	Acrimonious	(a)	hardened and insensitive
2.	Exuberant	(b)	unbelievable
3.	Affable	(c)	unprincipled
4.	Callous	(d)	lively
5.	Enormous	(e)	hostile
6.	Crucial	(f)	huge
7.	Vitriolic	(g)	friendly
8.	Spurious	(h)	sour or bitter (speech)
9.	Unscrupulous	(i)	critical
10.	Incredible	(j)	false

[B] Match the following:

	Words		*Meanings*
1.	Captious	(a)	rendered worn out, stale and unattractive because of over use.
2.	Adamant	(b)	useless
3.	Inevitable	(c)	that which causes severe and widespread effects

4. Transient (d) fault-finder
5. Invincible (e) hungry and extortionate
6. Jingoistic (f) temporary
7. Hackneyed (g) unavoidable
8. Ravenous (h) unconquerable
9. Futile (i) one who loves war
10. Drastic (j) stubbornly determined.

Answers

[A] 1-h; 2-d; 3-g; 4-a; 5-f; 6-i; 7-e; 8-j; 9-c; 10-b.

[B] 1-d; 2-j; 3-g; 4-f; 5-h; 6-i; 7-a; 8-e; 9-b; 10-c.

Calculate your marks

Give yourself +1 for each correct answer and add them up to get your score.

Marks obtained	***Remarks***
16-20	Excellent
14-15	Very good
12-13	Good
8-11	Fair
5-7	Average
Below 5	Poor.

Write the remark you got in the circle provided below in BOLD CAPITAL LETTER, with RED SKETCH PEN.

This is the remark our student got in this test which indicates how he/she is progressing through this course.

PART FOUR

Having a Good Vocabulary, makes you better than others!

ASSIGNMENT TEN. . . NOUNS.

Lesson One

[A] Pronounce the following words five times each

	Words	*Pronunciations*
1.	Apocalypse	ə`pokəlɪps
2.	Agony	`ægənɪ
3.	Paragon	`pærəgən
4.	Quintessence	kwɪn`tes(ə)ns
5.	Foray	`ʃoreɪ
6.	Flaw	flɔ:
7.	Milieu	mɪ`ljɜ:
8.	Coup d'etat	,ku:deɪ`ta:
9.	Calamity	kə`læmɪtɪ
10.	Turbulence	`tɜ:bjʊləns.

[B] Usage practice:

1 APOCALYPSE:

- **Meaning:** 'The Apocalypse' is God's revelation to St. John about vision of heaven and end of the earth. 'Apocalypse' is derived from 'the apocalypse', and means a tremendous destruction simulating the end of the world.
- **Sentence:** Misuse of nuke power would result in an apocalypse.

- **Your Sentence:** ....

....

2. **AGONY:**

- **Meaning:** Intense pain.
- **Sentence:** Every mother has to face the agony of child birth.
- **Your Sentence:** ....

....

3. **PARAGON:**

- **Meaning:** A model of perfection (in beauty, honesty or any virtue).
- **Sentence:** Aishwarya Rai is a paragon of beauty.
- **Your Sentence:** ....

....

4. **QUINTESSENCE:**

- **Meaning:** A perfect example of.
- **Sentence:** The movie 'Gandhi' has shown the quintessences of the true lives of freedom fighters.
- **Your Sentence:** ....

....

5. **FORAY:**

- **Meaning:** (1) A sudden, short-lasting attack.
- **Sentence:** (1) The violent foray bewildered the enemy troops.
- **Your Sentence:** ....

....

- **Meaning:** (2) First attempt (which is like a sudden, short-lasting attack), a successful.

- **Sentence:** (2) Actress Arundhati Roy surprised everyone by her highly successful foray in the writing field.
- **Your Sentence:** ....

....

6. FLAW:

- **Meaning:** Fault.
- **Sentence:** There was no flaw in the television.
- **Your Sentence:** ....

....

7. MILIEU:

- **Meaning:** Environment.
- **Sentence:** Internal milieu of a family has tremendous impact on development of children.
- **Your Sentence:** ....

....

8. COUP D'ETAT:

- **Meaning:** Sudden, violent overthrow of a government and illegal seizure of power.
- **Sentence:** The coup d'etat by Aurangzeb was strongly condemned in the whole empire.
- **Your Sentence:** ....

....

9. CALAMITY:

- **Meaning:** An unfortunate disaster.
- **Sentence:** Calamity fell on the poor villagers when the flood destroyed all their crops.
- **Your Sentence:** ....

....

10. TURBULENCE:

- **Meaning:** A violent agitation.
- **Sentence:** The turbulence of the storm wrecked the ship.
- **Your Sentence:** ....

....

[C] Match the following:

	Words		*Meaning*
1.	Apocalypse	(a)	fault
2.	Agony	(b)	a model of perfection
3.	Paragon	(c)	great destruction simulating the end of the world.
4.	Foray	(d)	severe pain
5.	Flaw	(e)	a sudden short-lasting attack

Answers: 1-c; 2-d; 3-b; 4-e; 5-a.

[D] Match the following:

	Words		*Meanings*
1.	Quintessence	(a)	environment
2.	Milieu	(b)	an unfortunate disaster
3.	Coup d'etat	(c)	violent agitation
4.	Calamity	(d)	a perfect example
5.	Turbulence	(e)	a sudden overthrow of government and illegal seizure of power

Answer: 1-d; 2-a; 3-e; 4-b; 5-c.

Lesson Two

[A] Pronounce the following words five times each

	Words	*Pronunciations*
1.	Anguish	\`æŋgwɪʃ
2.	Bestiality	,bestɪ\`ælɪtɪ
3.	Veracity	və\`ræsɪtɪ
4.	Apathy	\`æpəθI
5.	Discomfiture	dis\`kʌmfɪtʃə(r)
6.	Melancholy	′melənkəlɪ
7.	Elation	ɪ\`leɪʃ(ə)n
8.	Coup de Grace	,ku:də\`gra:s
9.	Nonpareil	,nonpə\`reIl

[B] Usage practice:

1 **ANGUISH:**

- **Meaning:** Anxiety, tense.
- **Sentence:** The anguish of the father could be seen on his face when he was told that his son had stolen some money.
- **Your Sentence:** ....

....

2 **BESTIALITY:**

- **Meaning:** Beast like cruelty.

- **Sentence:** History depicts numerous incidents of bestiality during the reign of Aurangzeb.
- **Your Sentence:** ....

....

3. VERACITY:

- **Meaning:** Truthfulness.
- **Sentence:** The inspector, checked the veracity of the criminal's statements very carefully.
- **Your Sentence:** ....

....

4. APATHY:

- **Meaning:** Lack of interest.
- **Sentence:** The child showed an apathy towards sports.
- **Your Sentence:** ....

....

5. DISCOMFITURE:

- **Meaning:** A feeling of uneasiness or confusion (while facing a particular thing, event, person, etc).
- **Sentence:** Anil develops a discomfiture on facing strangers.
- **Your Sentence:** ....

....

6. MELANCHOLY:

- **Meaning:** Sadness.
- **Sentence:** Her melancholy thawed away when she came in the arms of her husband.
- **Your Sentence:** ....

....

7. ELATION:

- **Meaning:** A state of being in pride and intense joy, (in highly elevated spirits).
- **Sentence:** The grand success in the examination filled him with elation.
- **Your Sentence:** ....

....

8. COUP DÉ GRACE:

- **Meaning:** Final and decisive blow.
- **Sentence:** The labour strike proved to be a coup dé grace on the textile industry.
- **Your Sentence:** ....

....

9. NONPAREIL:

- **Meaning:** Unparalleled.
- **Sentence:** The nonpareil charisma of the Indian women fascinated me.
- **Your Sentence:** ....

....

[C] Match the following:

Words	*Meaning*
1. Anguish	(a) beast like cruelty
2. Bestiality	(b) unparalleled
3. Veracity	(c) sadness
4. Apathy	(d) Uneasiness and confusion
5. Discomfiture	(e) anxiety, tense
6. Melancholy	(f) in highly elevated spirits
7. Elation	(g) final and decisive blow

8. Caup dé grace (h) truthfulness
9. Nonpareil (i) lack of interest.

Answers: 1-e; 2-a; 3-h; 4-i; 5-d; 6-c; 7-f; 8-g; 9-b.

[D] Write down the words you have learnt in this chapter in front of their meanings.

1. Intense pain: ....
2. Beast like cruelty: ....
3. Truthfulness: ....
4. Lack of interest: ....
5. Uneasiness mixed with confusion: ....
6. Sadness: ....
7. In highly elevated mood: ....
8. Final and decisive blow: ....
9. Unparalleled: ....

Answers: 1-anguish; 2-bestiality; 3-veracity; 4-apathy; 5-discomfiture; 6-melanchdy; 7-elation; 8-coup dé grace; 9-nonpareil.

Lesson Three

[A] Pronounce the following words five times each

Words	*Pronunciations*
1. Solitude	`solɪ,tju:d
2. Ambience	`æmbɪəns
3. Virtue	`vɜ:tju:
4. Conflagration	,konflə`greɪʃ(ə)n
5. Confidante	,konfɪ`dænt
6. Ally	`ælaɪ
7. Nostalgia	no`stældzɪə
8. Casuistry	,kæzju:`ɪstrɪ

[B] Usage practice:

1 SOLITUDE:

- **Meaning:** A lonely place.
- **Sentence:** People seek peace and solitude in times of distress.
- **Your Sentence:**

2. AMBIENCE:

- **Meaning:** Atmosphere or environment of a place.
- **Sentence:** The ambience of Bangalore is quite refreshing.

- **Your Sentence:** ....

  ....

3. VIRTUE:

- **Meaning:** A good quality.
- **Sentence:** Your virtues make you a lovable human being.
- **Your Sentence:** ....

  ....

4. CONFLAGRATION:

- **Meaning:** A huge, widespread fire causing much destruction.
- **Sentence:** Nuclear conflagration can ruin the whole world.
- **Your Sentence:** ....

  ....

5. CONFIDANTE:

- **Meaning:** Confidante is a female to whom one discloses one's secret private matters or affairs, and trusts her for not leaking those secrets to anyone.
- **Sentence:** My sister is my confidante.
- **Your Sentence:** ....

  ....

  (A male entrusted with such confidential matters is called confidant)

  [Don't get confused between confidant and confident. Confidant is a male to whom you reveal your secrets. While a confident person is one who has confidence or firm belief in one's ability to do something].

6. ALLY:

- **Meaning:** One who helps another in a work

- **Sentence:** The king depended on his allies to win the castle.
- **Your Sentence:** ....
....

7. **NOSTALGIA:**

- **Meaning:** Severe longing for the past; homesickness.
- **Sentence:** Unbearable nostalgia brought the London based Indian author back to India.
- **Your Sentence:** ....
....

8. **CASUISTRY:**

- **Meaning:** A clever but false reasoning.
- **Sentence:** Boys who have failed in the examination commonly come out with a remarkable casuistry.
- **Your Sentence:** ....
....

[C] Match the following:

Words		***Meanings***
1. Solitude	(a)	atmosphere; environment
2. Ambience	(b)	a huge fire that causes widespread destruction.
3. Virtue	(c)	a supporter
4. Conflagration	(d)	a lonely place
5. Confidante	(e)	a female entrusted with the knowledge of one's private matters.
6. Ally	(f)	a clever but false reasoning
7. Nostalgia	(g)	a good quality

8. Casuistry (h) homesickness.

Answers: 1-d; 2-a; 3-g; 4-b; 5-e; 6-c; 7-h; 8-f.

[D] Write the words you have learnt in this chapter in front of their meanings.

1. A lonely place: ....
2. Environment: ....
3. A good quality: ....
4. A huge fire causing great destruction: ....
5. A female entrusted with the knowledge of one's private matters: ....
6. A supporter: ....
7. Homesickness: ....
8. A clever but false reasoning: ....

Answers: 1-solitude; 2-ambience; 3-virtue; 4-conflagration; 5-confidante; 6-ally; 7-nostalgia; 8-casuistry.

Lesson Four

[A] Pronounce the following words five times each.

	Words	*Pronunciations*
1.	Prudence	\`pru:d(ə)ns
2.	Stint	stɪnt
3.	Bastinado	,bæstɪ\`neɪdo
4.	Rancour	\`ræŋkə(r)
5.	Rogue	rəʊg
6.	Ostentation	,osten'teɪʃ(ə)n
7.	Prejudice	\`predzʊdɪs
8.	Claustrophobia	,klɔ:strə\`fəʊbɪə
9.	Vengeance	'vendz(ə)ns

[B] Usage practice:

1. **PRUDENCE:**
   - **Meaning:** Watchfulness; vigilance.
   - **Sentence:** Prudence saves a person from embarrassment
   - **Your Sentence:** ....

     ....

2. **STINT:**
   - **Meaning:** (1) Restricted or scarce supply.
   - **Sentence:** This time the Government has distributed medicines to the poor with a stint.

- **Your Sentence:** ....

  ....

- **Meaning:** (2) A fixed amount of work given to someone.
- **Sentence:** "I have done my stint, sir," the soldier informed the commander.
- **Your Sentence:** ....

  ....

3. BASTINADO:

- **Meaning:** The punishment consisting of beating the soles of a person mercilessly by a stick.
- **Sentence:** The inspector inflicted a terrible bastinado on the criminal.
- **Your Sentence:** ....

  ....

4. RANCOUR:

- **Meaning:** (Deep seated) bitter hatred (eg. hatred of a slave toward his cruel master; hatred of a loser towards a competitor who always wins).
- **Sentence:** The unbearable rancour in the heart of the slave instigated him to murder his cruel master.
- **Your Sentence:** ....

  ....

5. ROGUE:

- **Meaning:** An immoral unprincipled person.
- **Sentence:** The girls got irritated by the indecent comments of the rogues in the classroom.
- **Your Sentence:** ....

  ....

6. OSTENTATION:

- **Meaning:** Pretentious show-off; gaudy display.
- **Sentence:** Ostentation has become common in the middle class families now-a-days.
- **Your Sentence:** ....

....

7. PREJUDICE:

- **Meaning:** Unreasonable (often harmful) preference; bias.
- **Sentence:** Prejudice in deciding the winners of the competition, resulted in tremendous resentment among competitors
- **Your Sentence:** ....

....

8. CLAUSTROPHOBIA:

- **Meaning:** Abnormal fear of closed space; (eg. fear of closed room; picture halls, etc.)
- **Sentence:** After ten years of imprisonment the prisoner developed claustrophobia.
- **Your Sentence:** ....

....

9. VENGEANCE:

- **Meaning:** Revenge.
- **Sentence:** Fire of vengeance burns in the hearts of the orphans whose parents were killed by the terrorists.
- **Your Sentence:** ....

....

[C] Match the following:

	Words		*Meanings*
1.	Prudence	(a)	deep seated hatred.
2.	Stint	(b)	fear of closed space.
3.	Bastinado	(c)	a preformed opinion.
4.	Rancour	(d)	watchfulness.
5.	Rogue	(e)	show-off.
6.	Ostentation	(f)	scarce supply.
7.	Prejudice	(g)	revenge.
8.	Claustrophobia	(h)	a punishment in which the soles are beaten mercilessly by a stick.
9.	Vengeance	(i)	an immoral, unprincipled person.

Answers: 1-d; 2-f; 3-h; 4-a; 5-i; 6-e; 7-c; 8-b; 9-g.

[D] Can you recall the words you have learnt in this chapter?

1. Pru ....
2. St ....
3. Ba ....
4. Ra ....
5. Ro ....
6. Os ....
7. Pre ....
8. Cl ....
9. Ve ....

Answers: 1-prudence; 2-stint; 3-bastinado; 4-rancour; 5-rogue; 6-ostentation; 7-prejudice; 8-claustrophobia; 9-vengeance.

Lesson Five

[A] Pronounce the following words five times each.

	Words	*Pronunciations*
1.	Predicament	prɪ`dikəmənt
2.	Libertine	`lɪbə,ti:n
3.	Effigy	`efɪdzɪ
4.	Homage	`homɪdz
5.	Homicide	`homɪ,saɪd
6.	Perfidy	`pɜ:fɪdɪ
7.	Surge	sɜ:dz
8.	Vendetta	ven`detə
9.	Catharsis	kə`θa:sɪs

[B] Usage practice:

1. PREDICAMENT:

- **Meaning:** A difficult, uncomfortable and embarrassing situation.
- **Sentence:** The failure in the examination landed him in a predicament.
- **Your Sentence:** ....

....

2. LIBERTINE:

- **Meaning:** A non-caring, immoral and licentious

person. [a person who loves liberty, does anything he like whether moral or immoral, and never cares about what impact his irresponsible actions are making on other people].

- **Sentence:** Many teenagers tend to become libertine, but soon they realize that they are on the wrong path.
- **Your Sentence:** ....

....

3. EFFIGY:

- **Meaning:** Model; image.
- **Sentence:** The agitated crowd burnt the effigy of the corrupt minister in the market.
- **Your Sentence:** ....

....

4. HOMAGE:

- **Meaning:** A feeling of respect and duty towards someone.
- **Sentence:** We all must pay homage to the freedom fighters of our country.
- **Your Sentence:** ....

....

5. HOMICIDE:

- **Meaning:** Murder of a human being.
- **Sentence:** Number of homicides are increasing at an alarming speed.
- **Your Sentence:** ....

....

6. PERFIDY:

- **Meaning:** Treachery, disloyalty.

- **Sentence:** Perfidy, in married life leads to divorce.
- **Your Sentence:** ....

....

7. **SURGE:**

- **Meaning:** A sudden, rapid rise.
- **Sentence:** The unexpected surge in prices has made living very difficult for the poor.
- **Your Sentence:** ....

....

8. **VENDETTA:**

- **Meaning:** Vendetta is a blood-thirsty enmity between two families, in which the family of a murdered person seeks revenge on the murderer, or his family.
- **Sentence:** Vendetta between the Luke and Raj families has taken many lives.
- **Your Sentence:** ....

....

9. **CATHARSIS:**

- **Meaning:** The release of strongly suppressed feelings, thereby relieving the person. This release may occur in the form of art, sculpture, writings, drama, even by speaking out one's mind openly.
- **Sentence:** The autobiography is an excellent piece of catharsis of the author.
- **Your Sentence:** ....

....

[C] Match the following:

	Words		*Meanings*
1.	Predicament	(a)	a feeling of respect and duty towards someone.
2.	Libertine	(b)	release of strongly suppressed emotions.
3.	Effigy	(c)	a difficult, uncomfortable and embarrassing situation
4.	Homage	(d)	treachery
5.	Homicide	(e)	a careless, immoral and licentious person
6.	Perfidy	(f)	killing of a human being
7.	Surge	(g)	blood thirsty enmity
8.	Vendetta	(h)	a model
9.	Catharsis	(i)	a sudden and rapid rise.

Answers: 1-c; 2-e; 3-h; 4-a; 5-f; 6-d; 7-i; 8-g; 9-b.

Lesson Six

[A] Pronounce the following words five times each

Words	*Pronunciations*
1. Boor	\`bʊə(r)
2. Booty	\`bu:tɪ
3. Bliss	blɪs
4. Adulation	ædjʊ\`leɪʃ(ə)n
5. Flippancy	\`ƒlɪpənsɪ
6. Incredulity	,ɪnkrɪ'dju:lɪtɪ
7. Lustre	\`lʌstə(r)
8. Chagrin	\`ʃægrɪn
9. Panache	pə\`næʃ

[B] Usage practice:

1 BOOR:

- **Meaning:** Rude, ill-mannered and insensitive person.
- **Sentence:** Meena hates her boor classmates who don't even know how to be polite to a girl.
- **Your Sentence:** ....

....

2 BOOTY:

- **Meaning:** Money or wealth looted in a war.
- **Sentence:** A big booty fell in the hands of the invaders in their battle against the Indian ruler.
- **Your Sentence:** ....

  ....

3. BLISS:

- **Meaning:** Perfect, heavenly happiness and peace.
- **Sentence:** Love was a bliss for Adam and Eve.
- **Your Sentence:** ....

  ....

4. ADULATION:

- **Meaning:** Flattery (done to gain some favours).
- **Sentence:** Ramesh indulges in a lot of adulation to gain favours from the officers.
- **Your Sentence:** ....

  ....

5. FLIPPANCY:

- **Meaning:** Frivolousness; lack of seriousness.
- **Sentence:** The husband got irritated by the flippancy of his wife's behaviour.
- **Your Sentence:** ....

  ....

6. INCREDULITY:

- **Meaning:** Disbelief.
- **Sentence:** (1) Everyone treated the news of spaceships landing on earth with incredulity.

  (2) Every child hates the incredulity of their parents towards their statements.

- **Your Sentence:** ....

 ....

7. LUSTRE:

- **Meaning:** Brilliance; glaze; shine.
- **Sentence:** I love the lustre of her eyes.
- **Your Sentence:** ....

 ....

8. CHAGRIN:

- **Meaning:** Deep seated sadness (which is often a result of humiliation or embarrassment)
- **Sentence:** The humiliation filled him with chagrin.
- **Your Sentence:** ....

 ....

9. PANACHE:

- **Meaning:** Pompous confidence and assertiveness with a lot of style and manners Just imagine such a person!)
- **Sentence:** Rahul tried to camouflage his inferiority complex with panache.
- **Your Sentence:** ....

 ....

[C] Match the following:

	Words		*Meanings*
1.	Boor	(a)	servile flattery
2.	Booty	(b)	deep seated sadness
3.	Bliss	(c)	rude ill-mannered and insensitive person
4.	Adulation	(d)	money looted in a war.

5. Flippancy (e) showing confidence and assertiveness with a pompous style and manners.
6. Incredulity (f) perfect happiness
7. Lusture (g) frivolousness
8. Chagrin (h) brilliance; shine
9. Panache (i) disbelief.

Answers: 1-c; 2-d; 3-f; 4-a; 5-g; 6-i; 7-h; 8-b; 9-e.

[D] Write the words you have learnt in this chapter in front of their meanings.

1. A rude, ill mannered and insensitive person: B..................................
2. Money looted in a war: B..................................
3. Perfect happiness: B..................................
4. Servile flattery: A..................................
5. Frivolousness: F..................................
6. Disbelief: I..................................
7. Brilliance: L..................................
8. Deep seated sadness: C..................................
9. Showing confidence and assertiveness, with pompous style and manners: P..................................

Answers: 1-boor; 2-booty; 3-bliss; 4-adulation; 5-flippancy; 6-incredulity; 7-lustre; 8-chagrin; 9-panache.

Lesson Seven

TEST YOUR PROGRESS

Revise exercise B of all the lessons discussed in this assignment, so that you may score well in this test too,

[A] Match the following:

	Words		*Meanings*
1.	Nostalgia	(a)	environment.
2.	Apocalypse	(b)	a lonely place.
3.	Milieu	(c)	model
4.	Rogue	(d)	anxiety
5.	Anguish	(e)	a female entrusted with the knowledge of one's private matters.
6.	Solitude	(f)	unprincipled person
7.	Conflagration	(g)	homesickness
8.	Confidante	(h)	a huge fire that causes much destruction
9.	Prudence	(i)	great destruction simulating the end of the world
10	Effigy	(j)	watchfulness; vigilance

[B] Match the following:

Words		*Meanings*
1. Rancour	(a)	murder of a human being.
2. Veracity	(b)	treachery.
3. Prejudice	(c)	deep seated bitter hatred.
4. Libertine	(d)	disbelief.
5. Homicide.	(e)	rude, ill mannered and insensitive person.
6. Perfidy	(f)	shine.
7. Surge	(g)	unreasonable preference.
8. Boor	(h)	truthfulness.
9. Incredulity	(i)	immoral, licentious, freedom loving person.
10. Lustre	(j)	sudden and rapid rise.

Answers

[A] 1-g; 2-i; 3-a; 4-f; 5-d; 6-b; 7-h; 8-e; 9-j; 10-c.

[B] 1-c; 2-h; 3-g; 4-i; 5-a; 6-b; 7-j; 8-e; 9-d; 10-f.

Calculate your marks:

Give yourself +1 per each correct answer, and add them upto get your score.

Marks obtained	*Remarks*
16-20	Excellent
14-15	Very good
12-13	Good
8-11	Fair
5-7	Average
Below 5	Poor

Write the remark you got in this test in the circle provided below with RED SKETCH PEN, in BOLD CAPITAL LETTERS.

This is the remarks our student got in this test which shows how he/she is progressing this course.

Assignment Test — Marks [illegible]

Write the remarks you got in this test in the circle provided below with RED SKETCH PEN in BOLD CAPITAL LETTERS

This will ensure that student gets instant feedback which shows how he/she is progressing in the course.

Good Vocabulary is the strongest foundation of success!

ASSIGNMENT ELEVEN. . . VERBS.

Lesson One

[A] Pronounce the following words five times each.

	Words	*Pronunciations*
1.	Protest	`prəʊtest
2.	Opt	opt
3.	Interact	,ɪntər`ækt
4.	Substantiate	səb`stænʃɪ,eɪt
5.	Raid	reɪd
6.	Actuate	`æktʃʊ,eɪt
7.	Overwhelm	,eʊvə`welm

[B] Usage practice:

1. PROTEST:

- **Meaning:** To declare one's objection, and demand a change.
- **Sentence:** All nations stood up to protest against nuclear test.
- **Your Sentence:** ....

....

2. OPT:

- **Meaning:** To choose.
- **Sentence:** Don't opt for a profession which you don't like.

- **Your Sentence:** ....

....

3. **INTERACT:**

- **Meaning:** To exchange actions with each other. [eg. if A writes a letter to B, and B answers that letter, we say A and B are interacting with each other].
- **Sentence:** In college, students get ample chance of interacting with each other.
- **Your Sentence:** ....

....

4. **SUBSTANTIATE:**

- **Meaning:** To add substance, or strength to.
- **Sentence:** (1) Your statement might substantiate the protest of the innocent man.

  (2) The principal took help of the bank to substantiate the financial condition of the college.
- **Your Sentence:** ....

....

5. **RAID:**

- **Meaning:** To make a surprising, short-lasting attack.
- **Sentence:** The Mongols raided India many times.
- **Your Sentence:** ....

....

6. **ACTUATE:**

- **Meaning:** To bring into action.
- **Sentence:** Raja Ram Mohan Roy actuated a big revolution in India.

- **Your Sentence:** ....

....

7. OVERWHELM:

- **Meaning:** To overpower; to crush.
- **Sentence:** Her tears overwhelmed my anger.
- **Your Sentence:** ....

....

[C] Match the following:

	Words		*Meanings*
1.	Protest	(a)	to add substance or strength to
2.	Opt	(b)	to make a surprising, short-lasting attack
3.	Interact	(c)	to over power.
4.	Substantiate	(d)	to declare one's objection
5.	Raid	(e)	to bring into action
6.	Actuate	(f)	to make a choice
7.	Overwhelm	(g)	to exchange actions with each other.

Answers: 1-d; 2-f; 3-g; 4-a; 5-b; 6-e; 7-c.

[D] Write the words you have learnt in this chapter in front of their meanings.

1. To declare one's objection: ....
2. To choose: ....
3. To exchange actions with each other: ....
4. To provide strength to: ....
5. To make a surprising attack: ....

6. To bring into action: ....

7. To overpower: ....

Answers: 1-protest; 2-opt; 3-interact; 4-substantiate; 5-raid; 6-actuate; 7-overwhelm.

Lesson Two

[A] Pronounce the following words five times each

	Words	*Pronunciations*
1.	Capsize	kæp`saɪz
2.	Derail	dɪ`reɪl
3.	Intervene	ˌɪntə`vi:n
4.	Prevail	prɪ`veɪl
5.	Reside	rɪ`zaɪd
6.	Mesmerize	`mezməˌraɪz
7.	Placate	plə`keɪt

[B] Usage practice:

1. CAPSIZE:

- **Meaning:** To overturn or overthrow accidentally (eg. a boat)
- **Sentence:** The storm capsized the fisherman's boat.
- **Your Sentence:** ....

....

2. DERAIL:

- **Meaning:** To make a train go off the rails.
- **Sentence:** Sahni express got derailed yesterday, causing 124 deaths.

- **Your Sentence:** ....

....

3. **INTERVENE:**

- **Meaning:** To interfere.
- **Sentence:** I had to intervene in their personal matters in order to stop them from taking divorce.
- **Your Sentence:** ....

....

4. **PREVAIL:**

- **Meaning:** To remain established [eg. disease prevails in epidemics, heat, prevails in deserts]
- **Sentence:** Let not crime prevail in your locality.
- **Your Sentence:** ....

....

5. **RESIDE:**

- **Meaning:** To live in.
- **Sentence:** Where do you reside?
- **Your Sentence:** ....

....

6. **MESMERIZE:**

- **Meaning:** To hold someone spell-bound or fascinated.
- **Sentence:** All the viewers were mesmerized by the beauty of the actress.
- **Your Sentence:** ....

....

7. **PLACATE:**

- **Meaning:** To pacify; to calm down.

- **Sentence:** Sunil presented flowers to his wife in order to placate her anger.
- **Your Sentence:** ....

....

[C] Match the following:

	Words		*Meanings*
1.	Capsize	(a)	to interfere
2.	Derail	(b)	to overturn accidentally.
3.	Intervene	(c)	to make a train go off the rails.
4.	Prevail	(d)	to calm down.
5.	Reside	(e)	to remain established
6.	Mesmerize	(f)	to live in
7.	Placate	(g)	to hold spell-bound.

Answers: 1-b; 2-c; 3-a; 4-e; 5-f; 6-g; 7-d.

[D] Write the words you have learnt in this chapter in front of their meanings.

1. To overturn accidentally: C ....
2. To make a train go off the rails: D ....
3. To interfere: I ....
4. To remain established: P ....
5. To live in: R ....
6. To hold spell-bound: M ....
7. To calm down: P ....

Answers: 1-capsize; 2-derail; 3-intervene; 4-prevail; 5-reside; 6-mesmerize; 7-placate.

Lesson Three

[A] Pronounce the following words five times each

	Words	*Pronunciations*
1.	Usher	\`ʌʃə(r)
2.	Mandate	\`mændeIt
3.	Trudge	trʌdz
4.	Appease	ə\`pi:z
5.	Liberate	\`lIbə,reIt
6.	Intimidate	In\`tImI,deIt

[B] Usage practice:

1. USHER:

- **Meaning:** To accompany people and show them their way.

  [Usher, the noun, means an officer who shows people the way to their seats in picture halls, functions, etc]

- **Sentence:** (1) "A medical student ushered us to your chamber, sir," a patient said to the doctor.

  (2) Parents usher their children to the best possible establishments.

- **Your Sentence:** ....

  ....

2 **MANDATE:**

- **Meaning:** To give authority to someone, and to make it essential for him to do the work.
- **Sentence:** The principal mandated the teachers to maintain strict discipline in the college.
- **Your Sentence:** ....

....

3. **TRUDGE:**

- **Meaning:** To walk tiredly, with heavy feet.
- **Sentence:** Sonal had to trudge all his way up the mountain to reach the temple.
- **Your Sentence:** ....

....

4. **APPEASE:**

- **Meaning:** To calm down by satisfying (thirst, desire, etc.)
- **Sentence:** The delicious food appeased my appetite.
- **Your Sentence:** ....

....

5. **LIBERATE:**

- **Meaning:** To set free.
- **Sentence:** The girl liberated all the birds from the cage.
- **Your Sentence:** ....

....

5. **INTIMIDATE:**

- **Meaning:** To subdue a person by filling him with fear; to make timid.

- **Sentence:** The criminal tried to intimidate the eye witness by showing him a dagger.
- **Your Sentence:** ....

....

[C] Match the following:

	Words		*Meanings*
1.	Usher	(a)	to give authority to someone and to make it essential for him to complete the work.
2.	Mandate	(b)	to set free
3.	Trudge	(c)	to accompany people and show them their way
4.	Appease	(d)	to subdue by filling with tear.
5.	Liberate	(e)	to walk with heavy, tired feet.
6.	Intimidate	(f)	to calm down by satisfying (thirst desire etc.).

Answers: 1-c; 2-a; 3-e; 4-f; 5-b; 6-d.

[D] Write down the words you have learnt in this chapter in front of their meanings.

1. To accompany people and show them their way:.......
2. To give authority to someone and make it necessary for him to perform something:....................................
3. To walk tiredly:..
4. To calm down by satisfying:..
5. To set free:..
6. To subdue by frightening:..

Answers: 1-usher; 2-mandate; 3-trudge; 4-appease; 5-liberate; 6-intimidate.

Lesson Four

[A] Speak aloud the following words five times each

	Words	*Pronunciations*
1.	Relish	\`relɪʃ
2.	Unveil	ʌn\`veɪl
3.	Anticipate	æn\`tɪsɪ,peɪt
4.	Wince	wɪns
5.	Instigate	\`ɪnstɪ,geɪt
6.	Wheedle	\`wi:d(ə)l

[B] Usage practice:

1. RELISH:

- **Meaning:** To like or enjoy something very much (e.g. food, drinks; the creams, coffee etc.).
- **Sentence:** (1) I relish the flavour of coffee.

  (2) My wife relishes ice creams.
- **Your Sentence:** ....

  ....

2 UNVEIL:

- **Meaning:** To remove the veil or cover of.

  [Veil is a piece of thin cloth that is used to cover the face.]
- **Sentence:** The enquiry unveiled startling secrets.

- **Your Sentence:** ....

  ....

3. **ANTICIPATE:**

- **Meaning:** To expect.
- **Sentence:** We anticipated victory but failed.
- **Your Sentence:** ....

  ....

4. **WINCE:**

- **Meaning:** To react to severe pain (usually it is a withdrawal type reaction)
- **Sentence:** (1) I winced in pain when a thorn pierced my sole.
- **Your Sentence:** ....

  ....

5. **INSTIGATE:**

- **Meaning:** To incite, provoke or start (an action, work, etc.).
- **Sentence:** (1) The rogues instigated a lot of criminal activities in the town

  (2) Menaka Gandhi has instigated a revolution in India to save wild life.
- **Your Sentence:** ....

  ....

6. **WHEEDLE:**

- **Meaning:** To persuade or manipulate gently and carefully.
- **Sentence:** The boy tried to wheedle Anita to elope with him, but she strictly refused.
- **Your Sentence:** ....

  ....

[C] Match the words in column A to their meanings in column B

Column A		*Column B*
1. Relish	(a)	to withdraw due to pain; to react due to pain (physical or emotional).
2. Unveil	(b)	to start by provoking.
3. Anticipate	(c)	to like or enjoy something intensely.
4. Wince	(d)	to remove the cover of
5. Instigate	(e)	to expect.
6. Wheedle	(f)	to give a surprising shock mixed with slight fear.
7. Startle	(g)	to persuade gently, carefully, and cunningly.

Answers: 1-c; 2-d; 3-e; 4-a; 5-b; 6-g; 7-f.

[D] Unite the words you have learnt in this chapter in front of their meanings.

1. To like or enjoy something immensely:........................
2. To remove the cover of: ....
3. To expect: ....
4. To react due to physical, mental or emotional agony:

   ....
5. To start something by provoking someone:..................
6. To persuade gently, carefully and cunningly:..............

   ....

Answers: 1-ɪelish; 2-unveil; 3-anticipate; 4-wince; 5-instigate; 6-wheedle.

Lesson Five

[A] Pronounce the following words five times each

	Words	*Pronunciations*
1.	Falter	\`foltə(r)
2.	Commence	kə\`mens
3.	Beckon	\`bekən
4.	Fortify	\`fɔ:tɪ,faɪ
5.	Scan	skæn
6.	Transcend	tra:n\`send
7.	Obfuscate	\`obfʌ,skeɪt

[B] Usage practice:

1 **FALTER:**

- **Meaning:** To become unsteady, (in one's actions), or stammer (in speech).
- **Sentence:** The boy faltered while answering in the classroom.

2 **COMMENCE:**

- **Meaning:** To begin.
- **Sentence:** The prayer commenced at 7:30 a.m. in the morning.
- **Your Sentence:** ....

....

3. BECKON:

- **Meaning:** To signal or give a hint to do something (the gesturing in a typical way; blinking eyes etc.).
- **Sentence:** My sister beckoned me not to disclose her secret.
- **Your Sentence:** ....

....

4. FORTIFY:

- **Meaning:** to strengthen; to make stronger (strong like a fort).
- **Sentence:** (1) The businessmen tried to fortify the security of his house by building a fence around it.

  (2) My son has fortified his financial condition by starting a new business.
- **Your Sentence:** ....

....

5. SCAN:

- **Meaning:** Examine or search carefully.
- **Sentence:** The investigator scanned the whole house to find the hidden gold.
- **Your Sentence:** ....

....

6. TRANSCEND:

- **Meaning:** To be or rise above the level of (knowledge, reasoning etc.).
- **Sentence:** Treatment of an AIDS patient transcends our imagination.
- **Your Sentence:** ....

....

- **Note:** 'Transcendental', the adjective form of the verb 'transcend', means something which is beyond experience or knowledge e.g. the supernatural or spiritual world.
- **Sentence:** The transcendental description of the strange behaviour of my friend (that he was under the control of a ghost) irritated me.
- **Your Sentence:** ....

....

7. OBFUSCATE:

- **Meaning:** (1) To hide; to hide in darkness; to make unclear or confusing.
- **Sentence:** The girls were trying to obfuscate the reality, after returning late to the hostel.
- **Your Sentence:** ....

....

- **Meaning (2):** Make one's mind dark, or confused.
- **Sentence (2):** (a) The unexpected failure obfuscated his mind.

  (b) The unexpected arrival of police obfuscated the mind of the thief.
- **Your Sentence:** ....

....

[C] Match the words in column A to thier meanings in column B.

Column A		*Column B*
1. Falter	(a)	to begin
2. Commence	(b)	to give signal or hint
3. Beckon	(c)	to become unsteady (in actions) or stammer (in speech).

4.	Fortify	(d)	to be above the level of (imagination, knowledge etc.)
5.	Scan	(e)	to make stronger
6.	Transcend	(f)	to hide; to make unclear or dark
7.	Obfuscate	(g)	to examine or search thoroughly and carefully.

Answers: 1-c; 2-a; 3-b; 4-e; 5-g; 6-d; 7-f.

[D] Write the words you have learnt in this chapter in front of their meanings given below:

1. To stammer: ....
2. To begin: ....
3. To give signal or hint: ....
4. To make stronger: ....
5. To examine or search carefully: ....
6. To be above the level of (knowledge or imagination):

   ....
7. To darken; to make unclear or confused: ....

Answers: 1-falter; 2-commence; 3-beckon; 4-fortify; 5-scan; 6-transcend; 7-obfuscate.

Lesson Six

[A] Pronounce the following words five times each

	Words	*Pronunciations*
1.	Acquiesce	,ækwIès
2.	Insinuate	In`sInjʊeIt
3.	Despise	dI`spaIz
4.	Impede	Im`pi:d
5.	Endear	In`dIə(r)
6.	Persist	pə`sIst
7.	Vindicate	`vIndI,keIt
8.	Gormandize	`gɔ:mən,daIz
9.	Fabricate	`fæbrI,keIt
10.	Engender	In`dzendə(r)

[B] Usage practice:

1. ACQUIESCE:

- **Meaning:** To gain or accept something without any complaint or objection.
- **Sentence:** (1) Sangeeta acquiesced the medical knowledge in five years.

  (2) The captain acquiesced his wounds in the dangerous battle.
- **Your Sentence:** ....

  ....

2 INSINUATE:

- **Meaning:** (1) To express or suggest indirectly; to give an indirect hints.
- **Sentence** (1): The nurse insinuated that the patient was insane.
- **Your Sentence:** ....
....
- **Meaning:** (2) To gain entry into (a powerful rank, a group, a family etc.) by careful manipulations.
- **Sentence:** (2) The detective managed to insinuate into the gang somehow.
- **Your Sentence:** ....
....

3. DESPISE:

- **Meaning:** To hate strongly.
- **Sentence:** I despise corruption.
- **Your Sentence:** ....
....

4. IMPEDE:

- **Meaning:** To disrupt, to slow down the progress of.
- **Sentence:** The competitors tried to impede Archana's progress, but failed.
- **Your Sentence:** ....
....

5. ENDEAR:

- **Meaning:** To make dear or loveable.
- **Sentence:** Bindu's innocence has endeared her to all us.

- **Your Sentence:** ....

  ....

6. **PERSIST:**

- **Meaning:** To remain established, or continue to stay (despite oppositions or trouble).
- **Sentence:** Arun persisted in the film industry despite the tough competition.
- **Your Sentence:** ....

  ....

7. **VINDICATE:**

- **Meaning:** To free someone from guilt or blame.
- **Sentence:** The court has vindicated Mr. Saxena from the charge of corruption.
- **Your Sentence:** ....

  ....

8. **GORMANDIZE:**

- **Meaning:** To eat greedily (like a pig).
- **Sentence:** The beggars gormandized all the food they received.
- **Your Sentence:** ....

  ....

9. **FABRICATE:**

- **Meaning:** To make (a false story, a lie etc.). This word has been derived from 'fabric' which is a knitted or woven cloth. So when we say that a person has 'fabricated' a story it means that he has made it, or 'woven' it up.
- **Sentence:** The student quickly fabricated an excuse for coming late.
- **Your Sentence:** ....

  ....

10. ENGENDER:

- **Meaning:** To produce, or give birth to.
- **Sentence:** Virtues like kindness and sincere service engender goodwill in society.
- **Your Sentence:** ....
....

[C] Match the words in column A to their meanings in column B.

Column A		*Column B*
1. Acquiesce	(a)	to weave (a false story etc.)
2. Insinuate	(b)	to hate
3. Despise	(c)	to make dear or loveable
4. Impede	(d)	to free from guilt or blame
5. Endear	(e)	to give birth to
6. Persist	(f)	to continue staying (despite difficulties)
7. Vindicate	(g)	to accept or gain without complaining
8. Gormandize	(h)	to disrupt the progress of
9. Fabricate	(i)	to eat greedily
10. Engender	(j)	to hint or suggest indirectly to gain entry by careful manipulators.

Answers: 1-g; 2-j; 3-b; 4-h; 5-c; 6-f; 7-d; 8-i; 9-a; 10-e.

[D] Try to recall the words you have learnt in this chapter. The meanings of the words have been given to help you recall them.

1. To accept without complaining:..
2. To gain entry by careful manipulations: ....

3. To hate: ....

4. To obstruct the progress of: ....

5. To make dear or loveable: ....

6. To continue to stay (despite obstacles): ....

7. To free (someone) from guilt or blame: ....

8. To eat greedily: ....

9. To make or 'weave' (a false story; lie etc.): ....

10. To give birth to: ....

Answers: 1-acquiesce; 2-insinuate; 3-despise; 4-impedes; 5-endear; 5-persist; 6-vindicate; 7-gormandize; 8-fabricate; 9-engender.

Lesson Seven

TEST YOUR PROGRESS

Quickly revise exercise B of all the lessons discussed in this assignment before taking this test so that you may get good marks.

[A] Match the words in column A to their meanings in column B.

Column A		*Column B*
1. Protest	(a)	to make a train go off the rails.
2. Opt	(b)	to walk tiredly, with heavy feet.
3. Raid	(c)	To love, like, or enjoy intensely.
4. Interact	(d)	to declare one's objections hoping to bring about a change.
5. Capsize	(e)	to exchange views.
6. Derail	(f)	to draw back shrink, or react in physical or emotional pain.
7. Trudge	(g)	to expect
8. Relish	(h)	to choose

9. Anticipate (i) to overturn (a boat) by accident.

10 Wince (j) to make a surprising attack.

[B] Match the following words to their meanings now.

1. Intervene (a) to make dear or loveable
2. Usher (b) to uncover
3. Appease (c) to interfere
4. Placate (d) to strengthen
5. Instigate (e) to hate
6. Unveil (f) to accompany people and show them their way
7. Falter (g) to stammer or become unsteady
8. Fortify (h) to calm down
9. Despise (i) to start (an action) by provoking or inciting.
10. Endear (j) to calm down (wager etc.) by satisfying the desire.

Answers:

[A]: 1-d; 2-h; 3-j; 4-e; 5-i; 6-a; 7-b; 8-c; 9-g; 10-f.

[B]: 1-c; 2-f; 3-j; 4-h; 5-i; 6-b; 7-g; 8-d; 9-e; 10-a.

Calculate your marks now.

Give yourself (+1) for each correct answer, then add up your marks to get your score.

Marks obtained	*Remarks*
16-20	Excellent
14-15	Very good
12-13	Good

Marks obtained	***Remarks***
8-11	Fair
5-7	Average
Below 5	Poor

Write down the remark you got in this test in the circle provided below with RED SKETCH PEN, and in BOLD CAPITAL LETTERS.

This is the remark our student got in this test which indicates how he/she is progressing through this course.

Each new word learnt is a step towards an effective personality!

ASSIGNMENT TWELVE. . . ADJECTIVES.

Lesson One

[A] Pronounce the following words five times each

	Words	*Pronunciations*
1.	Docile	\`dəʊsaɪl
2.	Deterrent	dɪ\`terənt
3.	Berserk	bə\`sɜ:k
4.	Relentless	rɪ\`lentlɪs
5.	Pliable	\`plaɪəb(ə)l
6.	Obstinate	\`obstɪnət
7.	Insolent	\`ɪnsələnt

[B] Usage practice:

1 DOCILE:

- **Meaning:** Submissive easy to tame or manage.
- **Sentence:** Everybody tries to take advantage of a docile person.
- **Your Sentence:** ....

....

2. DETERRENT:

- **Meaning:** One that has the power to deter, waver, or discourage a person by filling him with fear of whole world in looking with awe at consequences.
- **Sentence:** The whole world is looking with awe at the deterrent nuclear weapons.

- **Your Sentence:** ....

  ....

3. **BERSERK:**

- **Meaning:** Wild and outraged; frenzied.
- **Sentence:** The assination of Rajiv Gandhi made people go berserk.
- **Your Sentence:** ....

  ....

4. **RELENTLESS:**

- **Meaning:** Persistently inflexible, insistent and uncompromising.
- **Sentence:** The relentless efforts finally made him successful in the tough competitor.
- **Your Sentence:** ....

  ....

5. **PLIABLE:**

- **Meaning:** One who can be easily 'moulded' or influenced, according to the wishes of others, or circumstances.
- **Sentence:** In difficult times, people tend to become pliable.
- **Your Sentence:** ....

  ....

6. **OBSTINATE:**

- **Meaning:** Stubborn
- **Sentence:** An obstinate child has to be dealt with firmly.
- **Your Sentence:** ....

  ....

7. INSOLENT:

- **Meaning:** Offensively rude and insulting.
- **Sentence:** Insolent youths are too difficult to manage.
- **Your Sentence:** ....

....

[C] Match the words in column A to their meanings in column B.

Column A	*Column B*
1. Docile	(a) wild and frenzied.
2. Deterrent	(b) offensively rude and insulting.
3. Berserk	(c) easy to be 'moulded' or influenced.
4. Relentless	(d) stubborn.
5. Pliable	(e) something that deters or discourages others.
6. Obstinate	(f) submissive.
7. Insolent	(g) persistently inflexible and uncompromising.

Answers: 1-f; 2-e; 3-a; 4-g; 5-c; 6-d; 7-b.

[D] Try to recall the words you have learnt in this chapter. The meanings of the words have been given to help you recall them.

1. Submissive: ....
2. Something that deters or discourages a person: ....
3. Wild or frenzied: ....
4. Persistently inflexible and uncompromising: ....
5. Easy to be moulded or influenced: ....

6. Stubborn ....

7. Offensively rude and insulting: ....

Answers: 1-docile; 2-deterrent; 3-berserk; 4-relentless; 5-pliable; 6-obstinate; 7-insolent.

Lesson Two

[A] Speak aloud the following words ten times each.

	Words	*Pronunciations*
1.	Aggrieved	ə`gri:vd
2.	Esoteric	`i:səʊ`terɪk
3.	Obdurate	`obdjʊrət
4.	Obsequious	əb`si:kwɪəs
5.	Obsolete	'obsə,li:t
6.	Scurrilous	'skʌrɪləs
7.	Diligent	'dɪlɪdz(ə)nt

[B] Usage practice:

1. AGGRIEVED:

- **Meaning:** Unjustly injured; one having grievances.
- **Sentence:** The aggrieved citizens, protest against the hike in prices.
- **Your Sentence:** ....

....

2. ESOTERIC:

- **Meaning:** It is something very complex, which can be understood only by people who have special knowledge on expertise. It is beyond the understanding of ordinary people.
- **Sentence:** Some writers still prefer to write in esoteric style.

- **Your Sentence:** ....
....

3. **OBDURATE:**
   - **Meaning:** Stubborn:
   - **Sentence:** Her obdurate behaviour made her very unpopular among friends.
   - **Your Sentence:** ....
   ....

4. **OBSEQUIOUS:**
   - **Meaning:** Slavish; (person or behaviour).
   - **Sentence:** Julius Caesar hated the obsequious flattery of Cassius.
   - **Your Sentence:** ....
   ....

5. **OBSOLETE:**
   - **Meaning:** Outdated.
   - **Sentence:** The theory, that diseases are caused by evil spirits, has become obsolete.
   - **Your Sentence:** ....
   ....

6. **SCURRILOUS:**
   - **Meaning:** Indecent and abusive.
   - **Sentence:** Rogues passed scurrilous remarks on the girls.
   - **Your Sentence:** ....
   ....

7. **DILIGENT:**
   - **Meaning:** Hard working.
   - **Sentence:** Diligent boys always succeed in their exams.

- **Your Sentence:** ....

....

[C] Match the words in column A to their meanings in column B.

	Column A		*Column B*
1.	Aggrieved	(a)	outdated.
2.	Esoteric	(b)	hard working.
3.	Obdurate	(c)	indecent and abusive.
4.	Obsequious	(d)	too difficult to be understood by ordinary people.
5.	Obsolete	(e)	humble and cringing person (like a slave).
6.	Scurrilous	(f)	having grievances; unjustly hurt or injured.
7.	Diligent	(g)	stubborn and resistant to persuasion.

Answers: 1-f; 2-d; 3-g; 4-e; 5-a; 6-c; 7-b.

[D] Try to recall the words you have learnt in this chapter. The meanings of the words have been given to help you recall them.

1. One having grievances:..
2. Too difficult to be understood by ordinary people:....
3. Stubborn and resistant to persuasion:...........................
4. A humble and cringing (person or behaviour):............
5. Outdated: ....
6. Indecent and abusive: ....
7. Hard working:...

Answers: 1-aggrieved; 2-esoteric; 3-obdurate; 4-obsequious; 5-obsolete; 6-scurrilous; 7-diligent.

Lesson Three

[A] Pronounce the following words five times each.

	Words	*Pronunciations*
1.	Anonymous	ə`nonɪməs
2.	Arable	`ærəb(ə)l
3.	Aquiline	`ækwɪ,laɪn
4.	Archaic	ɑː`keɪɪk
5.	Arduous	`ɑːdjuːəs
6.	Ardent	`ɑːd(ə)nt
7.	Altruistic	,æltruː`ɪstɪk

[B] Usage practice:

1. ANONYMOUS:
   - **Meaning:** One whose owner's name is not known, e.g. if you get a letter whose sender's name "is not known, then the letter is an anonymous letter."
   - **Sentence:** The police received information about the criminal by an anonymous letter.
   - **Your Sentence:** ....

     ....

2. ARABLE:
   - **Meaning:** Well ploughed, and this well suited for growing crops.

- **Sentence:** Arable fields yield better crops.
- **Your Sentence:** ....

....

3. AQUILINE:

- **Meaning:** Of or like an eagle, e.g. If a nose is described as aquiline, it means it is curved like an eagle's beak.
- **Sentence:** The witch quivered her aquiline nose.
- **Your Sentence:** ....

....

4. ARCHAIC:

- **Meaning:** Something that belongs to historical times.
- **Sentence:** The archaic manuscripts are invaluable.
- **Your Sentence:** ....

....

5. ARDUOUS:

- **Meaning:** Very difficult.
- **Sentence:** It is easy for superman to do any arduous task.
- **Your Sentence:** ....

....

6. ARDENT:

- **Meaning:** Burning (with desire, enthusiasm etc); enthusiastic.
- **Sentence:** My girl has an ardent desire to become a good administrator.
- **Your Sentence:** ....

....

7. ALTRUISTIC:

- **Meaning:** A person who is engaged in welfare of people without any selfishness.
- **Sentence:** The altruistic nature of Mahatma Gandhi made him the leader of common people.
- **Your Sentence:** ....

....

[C] Match the words in column A to their meanings in column B

Column A		*Column B*
1. Anonymous	(a)	burning (with enthusiasm etc).
2. Arable	(b)	well ploughed, and well suited for growing crops.
3. Aquiline	(c)	one who has an unselfish concern for the welfare of people.
4. Archaic	(d)	too difficult or hard.
5. Arduous	(e)	one whose owner's name is not known; or something which is not claimed by any named person.
6. Ardent	(f)	belonging to historical times or antiquity.
7. Altruistic	(g)	like an eagle; or of an eagle.

Answers: 1-e; 2-b; 3-g; 4-f; 5-d; 6-a; 7-c.

[D] Write down the words you have learnt in this chapter in front of their meanings given below :

1. Having no named owner:..

2. Well ploughed, and thus well suited to grow crops:

   ....

3. Like an eagle: ....
4. Belonging to antiquity or historical times:....................
5. Too difficult or hard: ....
6. Burning (with enthusiasm, desire etc.): ....
7. One who does welfare of other's without any selfishness: ....

Answers: 1-anonymous; 2-arable; 3-aquiline; 4-archaic; 5-arduous; 6-ardent; 7-altruistic.

Lesson Four

[A] Speak aloud the following words ten times each.

	Words	*Pronunciations*
1.	Celestial	sɪ`lestiəl
2.	Charismatic	,kærɪz`mætɪk
3.	Ebullient	ɪ`bʌlɪənt
4.	Ecstatic	ɪk`stætɪk
5.	Eerie	`ɪərɪ
6.	Pusillanimous	,pju:sɪ`lænɪməs
7.	Solicitous	sə`lɪsɪtəs

[B] Usage practice:

1. **CELESTIAL:**
   - **Meaning:** Heavenly bodies (planets, satellites etc.);
   - **Sentence:** Astrologers are always interested in the movements of celestial bodies.
   - **Your Sentence:** ....

     ....

2. CHARISMATIC:
   - **Meaning:** Having great attractive and influencial powers.
   - **Sentence:** A prime minister should have a charismatic personality.

- **Your Sentence:** ....

....

3. **EBULLIENT:**

- **Meaning:** Boiling (with excitement eagerness or interest)
- **Sentence:** It was very nice to see the ebullient spirit of the social workers.
- **Your Sentence:** ....

....

4. **ECSTATIC:**

- **Meaning:** Ecstasy is the state of intense excitement and pleasure.
- **Sentence:** Children became ecstatic on meeting their grand mother.
- **Meaning:** (2) Something that gives such an intense excitement, satisfaction and joy (like a kiss; embrace etc.).
- **Sentence:** (2) She received an ecstatic kiss from her husband.
- **Your Sentence:** ....

....

5. **EERIE:**

- **Meaning:** Strange, frightening and mysterious.
- **Sentence:** (1) The eerie atmosphere of the old castle made her tremble with fear.
- **Your Sentence:** ....

....

6. **PUSILLANIMOUS:**

- **Meaning:** Cowardly.

- **Sentence:** The pusillanimous nature of the youth made in easier for his rivals to subdue him.
- **Your Sentence:** ....

....

7. **SOLICITOUS:**

- **Meaning:** That which causes welfare.
- **Sentence:** The solicitous nature of the social worker endeared him to the villagers.
- **Your Sentence:** ....

....

[C] Match the words in column A to their meanings in column B.

	Column A		*Column B*
1.	Celestial	(a)	boiling with interest or eagerness
2.	Charismatic	(b)	strange, frightening and mysterious
3.	Ebullient	(c)	one who intends to do much welfare of others
4.	Ecstatic	(d)	heavenly
5.	Eerie	(e)	in a state of intense excitement and delight
6.	Pusillanimous	(f)	having great power to attract and delight.
7.	Solicitous	(g)	cowardly.

Answers: 1-d; 2-f; 3-a; 4-e; 5-b; 6-g; 7-c.

[D] Write the words you have learnt in this chapter in front of their meanings given below:

1. Heavenly: ....

2. Having great power to attract and influence others:

   ....

3. Boiling with excitement, eagerness or interest:............
4. Intense pleasure (like a kiss, embrace etc.):...................
5. Strange, frightening and mysterious:.............................
6. Cowardly:..
7. One who intends to do welfare of others:.......................

Answers: 1-celestial; 2-charismatic; 3-ebullient; 4-ecstatic; 5-eerie; 6-pusillanimous; 7-solicitous.

Lesson Five

[A] Speak aloud the following words ten times each.

	Words	*Pronunciations*
1.	Queasy	`kwi:zɪ
2.	Querulous	`kwerʊləs
3.	Haggard	`hægəd
4.	Halcyon	`hælsɪən
5.	Salient	`seɪlɪənt
6.	Salubrious	sə`lu:brɪəs
7.	Rampant	`ræmpənt

[B] Usage practice:

1. **QUEASY:**
   - **Meaning:** Having an uneasy feeling, as if one is going to vomit.
   - **Sentence:** My little sister always starts feeling queasy when she goes by a bus.
   - **Your Sentence:** ....

     ....

2. **QUERULOUS**
   - **Meaning:** An irritable, complaining, and quarreling type of person.
   - **Sentence:** I really fear my querulous wife.

- **Your Sentence:** ....

  ....

3. HAGGARD:

- **Meaning:** One who looks ill tired and worn out.
- **Sentence:** "What a haggard you are!," the customer shouted when the tired looking manager refused to do his work.
- **Your Sentence:** ....

  ....

4. HALCYON:

- **Meaning:** Happy and peaceful.
- **Sentence:** "I still remember those halcyon days!" The nostalgic poet sighed.
- **Your Sentence:** ....

  ....

5. SALIENT:

- **Meaning:** Very important, prominent highly noticeable.
- **Sentence:** (1) The salient features of the textbook are printed on its cover.
- **Your Sentence:** ....

  ....

6. SALUBRIOUS:

- **Meaning:** Good for health.
- **Sentence:** Morning exercises are enjoyed in the salubrious environment of the park.
- **Your Sentence:** ....

  ....

7. RAMPANT:

- **Meaning:** Widespread, well established and progressive.
- **Sentence:** "Corruption is rampant nowadays. How can our country progress!" a man shouted in frustration.
- **Your Sentence:** ....

....

[C] Match the words in column A to their meanings in column B.

Column A	*Column B*
1. Queasy	(a) looking ill and tired
2. Querulous	(b) very important, highly prominent and noticeable
3. Haggard	(c) good for health
4. Halcyon	(d) having an uneasy feeling, as if one is going to vomit.
5. Salient	(e) well established widespread and rapidly progressive
6. Salubrious	(f) irritable and quarreling type of person
7. Rampant	(g) happy and peaceful.

Answers: 1-d; 2-f; 3-a; 4-g; 5-b; 6-c; 7-e.

[D] Try to recall the words you have learnt in this chapter. The meanings of the words have been given to help you do that.

1. Having an uneasy feeling, as if one is going to vomit:

   ....

2. Irritable and quarreling type of person: ....
3. Looking ill and tired: ....

4. Happy and peaceful: ....

5. Very important, highly prominent and noticeable:

   ....

6. Good for health: ....

7. Widespread, well established and progressing rapidly:

   ....

Answers: 1-queasy; 2-querulous; 3-haggard; 4-halcyon; 5-salient; 6-salubrious; 7-rampant.

Lesson Six

[A] Speak aloud the following words ten time each.

	Words	*Pronunciations*
1.	Heinous	\`heɪnəs/\`hi:nəs
2.	Hilarious	hɪ\`leərɪəs
3.	Refractory	ri\`fræktərɪ
4.	Refulgent	rɪ\`fʌldz(ə)nt
5.	Tortuous	\`tɒ:tjʊəs
6.	Sinister	\`sɪnɪstə(r)
7.	Excruciating	ik\`skru:ʃɪ,eɪtɪŋ
8.	Lugubrious	lu:\`gu:brɪəs
9.	Ambitious	æm\`bɪʃəs

[B] Usage practice:

1 HEINOUS:

- **Meaning:** Wicked and evil: (like a Jackab).
- **Sentence:** The heinous crime made my legs tremble.
- **Your Sentence:** ....

....

2. HILARIOUS:

- **Meaning:** Very funny, jocular.
- **Sentence:** I love hilarious movies.

- **Your Sentence:** ....

  ....

3. **REFRACTORY:**

- **Meaning:** Too resistant to be treated or managed.
- **Sentence:** Tuberculosis disease, if not treated properly, becomes refractory.
- **Your Sentence:** ....

  ....

4. **REFULGENT:**

- **Meaning:** Shining brilliantly.
- **Sentence:** (1) The refulgent jewellery attracted attention.

  (2) "Which shoe-polish do you use. Rohit? your shoes are so refulgent!", Sonu exclaimed.
- **Your Sentence:** ....

  ....

5. **TORTUOUS:**

- **Meaning:** Full of twists and turns.
- **Sentence:** Wish I could enter the tortuous burrows of the cute rabbits!.
- **Your Sentence:** ....

  ....

6. **SINISTER:**

- **Meaning:** Evil, threatening, and suggestive of harm.
- **Sentence:** (1) The sinister crow warned Mr. Snow that a storm would come soon to say hello!.

  (2) "Beware of that sinister jackal!," the priest warned.

- **Your Sentence:** ....
....

7. EXCRUCIATING:

- **Meaning:** That which give severe pain, making a person feel very very uneasy.
- **Sentence:** The excruciating pain of appendicitis was too hard to tolerate.
- **Your Sentence:** ....
....

8. LUGUBRIOUS:

- **Meaning:** Sad; gloomy.
- **Sentence:** "Look at those lugubrious faces. They seem to have lost their world!," the girl mocked at the gloomy boys.
- **Your Sentence:** ....
....

9. AMBITIOUS:

- **Meaning:** One who aims to achieve very high goals; one who has an intense desire to succeed and get high position and reputation.
- **Sentence:** Ambitious and hard-working students are sure to achieve the highest possible goals.
- **Your Sentence:** ....
....

[C] Match the words in column A to their meaning in column B.

Column A	*Column B*
1. Heinous	(a) to resistant to cure or manage.
2. Hilarious	(b) shining brilliantly.

3.	Refractory	(c)	full of twists and turns.
4.	Refulgent	(d)	evil and threatening.
5.	Tortuous	(e)	wicked and evil (like a jackal).
6.	Sinister	(f)	gloomy.
7.	Excruciating	(g)	very funny.
8.	Lugubrious	(h)	one who aims to achieve high goals.
9.	Ambitious	(i)	severe and very uncomfortable (pain).

Answers: 1-e; 2-g; 3-a; 4-b; 5-c; 6-d; 7-i; 8-f; 9-h.

[D] Try to recall the words you have learnt in this chapter. The meanings of the words have been given to help you recall them.

1. Wicked and evil (like a jackal): ....
2. Very funny or jocular: ....
3. Too resistant to be treated or managed: ....
4. Shining brilliantly: ....
5. Full of twists and turns: ....
6. Evil and threatening: ....
7. Severe, much uncomfortable: ....
8. Gloomy: ....
9. One who aims to achieve high goals: ....

Answers: 1-heinous; 2-hilarious; 3-refractory; 4-refulgent; 5-tortuous; 6-sinister; 7-excruciating; 8-lugubrious; 9-ambitious.

Lesson Seven

TEST YOUR PROGRESS

Revise Exercise B of all the chapters discussed in this 'step twelve' before taking this test, so that you may get a prestigious grade this time too.

[A] Match the following words in column A to their meanings in column B.

	Column A		*Column B*
1.	Obstinate	(a)	one that continues incessantly, is persistent and uncompromising.
2.	Relentless	(b)	burning with eagerness interest.
3	Obsolete	(c)	severe and uncomfortable (especially pain).
4.	Aggrieved	(d)	boiling with enthusiasm; excitement, etc.
5.	Ardent	(e)	good for health.
6.	Pusillanimous	(f)	stubborn.
7.	Ebullient	(g)	very funny; full of comedy.
8.	Salubrious	(h)	outdated.
9.	Hilarious	(i)	cowardly.
10.	Excruciating	(j)	one having grievances.

[B] Match the following:

1. Obdurate	(a) like an eagle.
2. Altruistic	(b) strange, frightening and mysterious.
3. Aquiline	(c) having great power of attracting and influencing others.
4. Arduous	(d) stubborn and resistant to persuasion.
5. Eerie	(e) wicked and evil. (like a jackal)
6. Charismatic	(f) one who thinks a lot about welfare of others, but for no selfish gains.
7. Halcyon	(g) Evil, threatening and suggestive of harm.
8. Heinous	(h) gloomy.
9. Sinister	(i) too hard or difficult.
10. Lugubrious	(j) happy and peaceful.

Check your answers now-

Answers: **[A]:** 1-f; 2-a; 3-h; 4-j; 5-b; 6-i; 7-d; 8-e; 9-g; 10-c.

[B]: 1-d; 2-f; 3-a; 4-i; 5-b; 6-c; 7-j; 8-e; 9-g; 10-h.

Calculate your marks

Give yourself one mark for each answer marked correctly, then add them up to get your total score.

Marks obtained	***Remarks***
16-20	Excellent
14-15	Very good
12-13	Good

Marks obtained	***Remarks***
8-11	Fair
5-7	Average
Below 5	Poor

Write the remark you got in this test in the circle provided below. Write it in BOLD CAPITAL LETTERS with RED SKETCH PEN.

This is the remarks our student got in this test which indicates how he/she is progressing through this course.

Index

WORD — ASSIGNMENT NUMBER — CHAPTER NUMBER

SEQUENCE

[B]

[C]

[S]

[T]

EPILOGUE

Dear Students,

Congratulations for completing this book. Now you have the greatest impressive power at your finger tips. But I must tell you one thing—no power lasts forever unless you maintain it properly. So please keep on revising this book at least once in a year, if you want to remain on top.

You can do more vocabulary books in your leisure hours. You can read 'six weeks to words of power' written by Wilfred Funk, or 'Thirty days to a more powerful vocabulary' written by Norman Lewis and Wilfred Funk.

Wish you all the best

Yours

Shailendra